ATHEISM IN PAGAN ANTIQUITY

ATHEISM IN
PAGAN ANTIQUITY

BY

A. B. DRACHMANN

PROFESSOR OF CLASSICAL PHILOLOGY IN THE UNIVERSITY OF COPENHAGEN

ARES PUBLISHERS INC.
CHICAGO   MCMLXXVII

Unchanged Reprint of the Edition:
London 1922
ARES PUBLISHERS INC.
612 N. Michigan Avenue
Chicago, Illinois 60611
Printed in the United States of America
International Standard Book Number:
0-89005-201-8

PREFACE

THE present treatise originally appeared in Danish as a University publication (*Kjøbenhavns Universitets Festskrift*, November 1919). In submitting it to the English public, I wish to acknowledge my profound indebtedness to Mr. G. F. Hill of the British Museum, who not only suggested the English edition, but also with untiring kindness has subjected the translation, as originally made by Miss Ingeborg Andersen, M.A. of Copenhagen, to a painstaking and most valuable revision.

For an account of the previous treatments of the subject, as well as of the method employed in my investigation, the reader is referred to the introductory remarks which precede the Notes.

A. B. DRACHMANN.

CHARLOTTENLUND,
July 1922.

CONTENTS

vii

CHAPTER IV

CHAPTER V

CHAPTER VI

CHAPTER VII

CONTENTS

CHAPTER VIII

CHAPTER IX

ATHEISM IN PAGAN ANTIQUITY

INTRODUCTION

THE present inquiry is the outcome of a request to write an article on " Atheism " for a projected dictionary of the religious history of classical antiquity. On going through the sources I found that the subject might well deserve a more comprehensive treatment than the scope of a dictionary would allow. It is such a treatment that I have attempted in the following pages.

A difficulty that occurred at the very beginning of the inquiry was how to define the notion of atheism. Nowadays the term is taken to designate the attitude which denies every idea of God. Even antiquity sometimes referred to atheism in this sense ; but an inquiry dealing with the history of religion could not start from a definition of that kind. It would have to keep in view, not the philosophical notion of God, but the conceptions of the gods as they appear in the religion of antiquity. Hence I came to define atheism in Pagan antiquity as the point of view which *denies the existence of the ancient gods*. It is in this sense that the word will be used in the following inquiry.

Even though we disregard philosophical atheism, the definition is somewhat narrow; for in antiquity mere denial of the existence of the gods of popular belief was not the only attitude which was designated as atheism. But it has the advantage of starting from the conception of the ancient gods that may be said to have finally prevailed. In the sense in which the word is used here we are nowadays all of us atheists. We do not believe that the gods whom the Greeks and the Romans worshipped and believed in exist or have ever existed ; we hold them to be productions of the human imagination to which nothing real corresponds. This view has nowadays become so ingrained in us and appears so self-evident, that we find it difficult to imagine that it has not been prevalent through long ages ; nay, it is perhaps a widely diffused assumption that even in antiquity educated and unbiased persons held the same view of the religion of their people as we do. In reality both assumptions are erroneous: our " atheism " in regard to ancient paganism is of recent date, and in antiquity itself downright denial of the existence of the gods was a comparatively rare phenomenon. The demonstration of this fact, rather than a consideration of the various intermediate positions taken up by the thinkers of antiquity in their desire to avoid a complete rupture with the traditional ideas of the gods, has been one of the chief purposes of this inquiry.

Though the definition of atheism set down here might seem to be clear and unequivocal, and though I have tried to adhere strictly to it, cases have unavoidably occurred that were difficult to classify.

The most embarrassing are those which involve a reinterpretation of the conception of the gods, *i.e.* which, while acknowledging that there is some reality corresponding to the conception, yet define this reality as essentially different from it. Moreover, the acknowledgment of a certain group of gods (the celestial bodies, for instance) combined with the rejection of others, may create difficulties in defining the notion of atheism ; in practice, however, this doctrine generally coincides with the former, by which the gods are explained away. On the whole it would hardly be just, in a field of inquiry like the present, to expect or require absolutely clearly defined boundary-lines ; transition forms will always occur.

The persons of whom it is related that they denied the existence of the ancient gods are in themselves few, and they all belong to the highest level of culture ; by far the greater part of them are simply professional philosophers. Hence the inquiry will almost exclusively have to deal with philosophers and philosophical schools and their doctrines ; of religion as exhibited in the masses, as a social factor, it will only treat by exception. But in its purpose it is concerned with the history of religion, not with philosophy ; therefore—in accordance with the definition of its object—it will deal as little as possible with the purely philosophical notions of God that have nothing to do with popular religion. What it aims at illustrating is a certain— if you like, the negative—aspect of ancient religion. But its result, if it can be sufficiently established, will not be without importance for the understanding of the positive religious sense of antiquity. If you want to obtain some idea of the hold a certain religion had on its adherents, it is not amiss to know something about the extent to which it dominated even the strata of society most exposed to influences that went against it.

It might seem more natural, in dealing with atheism in antiquity, to adopt the definition current among the ancients themselves. That this method would prove futile the following investigation will, I hope, make sufficiently evident ; antiquity succeeded as little as we moderns in connecting any clear and unequivocal idea with the words that signify " denial of God." On the other hand, it is, of course, impossible to begin at all except from the traditions of antiquity about denial and deniers. Hence the course of the inquiry will be, first to make clear what antiquity understood by denial of the gods and what persons it designated as deniers, and then to examine in how far these persons were atheists in our sense of the word.

CHAPTER I

ATHEISM and atheist are words formed from Greek roots and with Greek derivative endings. Nevertheless they are not Greek; their formation is not consonant with Greek usage. In Greek they said *atheos* and *atheotes*; to these the English words ungodly and ungodliness correspond rather closely. In exactly the same way as ungodly, *atheos* was used as an expression of severe censure and moral condemnation; this use is an old one, and the oldest that can be traced. Not till later do we find it employed to denote a certain philosophical creed; we even meet with philosophers bearing *atheos* as a regular surname. We know very little of the men in question; but it can hardly be doubted that *atheos*, as applied to them, implied not only a denial of the gods of popular belief, but a denial of gods in the widest sense of the word, or Atheism as it is nowadays understood.

In this case the word is more particularly a philosophical term. But it was used in a similar sense also in popular language, and corresponds then closely to the English " denier of God," denoting a person who denies the gods of his people and State. From the popular point of view the interest, of course, centred in those only, not in the

2

exponents of philosophical theology. Thus we find the word employed both of theoretical denial of the gods (atheism in our sense) and of practical denial of the gods, as in the case of the adherents of monotheism, Jews and Christians.

Atheism, in the theoretical as well as the practical sense of the word, was, according to the ancient conception of law, always a crime ; but in practice it was treated in different ways, which varied both according to the period in question and according to the more or less dangerous nature of the threat it offered to established religion. It is only as far as Athens and Imperial Rome are concerned that we have any definite knowledge of the law and the judicial procedure on this point ; a somewhat detailed account of the state of things in Athens and Rome cannot be dispensed with here.

In the criminal law of Athens we meet with the term *asebeia*—literally : impiety or disrespect towards the gods. As an established formula of accusation of *asebeia* existed, legislation must have dealt with the subject ; but how it was defined we do not know. The word itself conveys the idea that the law particularly had offences against public worship in view ; and this is confirmed by the fact that a number of such offences — from the felling of sacred trees to the profanation of the Eleusinian Mysteries—were treated as *asebeia*. When, in the next place, towards the close of the fifth century B.C., free-thinking began to assume forms which seemed dangerous to the religion of the State, theoretical denial of the gods was also included under *asebeia*. From about the beginning of the Peloponnesian War to the close of the fourth century B.C., there are on record a number of prosecutions of philosophers who were tried and condemned for denial of the gods. The indictment seems in most cases—the trial of Socrates is the only one of which we know details—to have been on the charge of *asebeia*, and the procedure proper thereto seems to have been employed, though there was no proof or assertion of the accused having offended against public worship ; as to Socrates, we know the opposite to have been the case ; he worshipped the gods like any other good citizen. This extension of the conception of *asebeia* to include theoretical denial of the gods no doubt had no foundation in law ; this is amongst other things evident from the fact that it was necessary, in order to convict Anaxagoras, to pass a special public resolution in virtue of which his freethinking theories became indictable. The law presumably dated from a time when theoretical denial of the gods lay beyond the horizon of legislation. Nevertheless, in the trial of Socrates it is simply taken for granted that denial of the gods is a capital crime, and that not only on the side of the prosecution, but also on the side of the defence : the trial only turns on a question of fact, the legal basis is taken for granted. So inveterate, then, at this time was the conception of the unlawful nature of the denial of the gods among the people of Athens.

In the course of the fourth century B.C. several philosophers were accused of denial of the gods or blasphemy ; but after the close of the century we hear no more of such trials. To be sure, our knowledge of the succeeding centuries, when Athens was but a provincial town, is far less copious than of the days of its greatness ; nevertheless, it is beyond doubt that the practice in regard to theoretical denial of the gods was changed. A philosopher like Carneades, for instance, might, in view of his sceptical standpoint, just as well have been convicted of *asebeia* as Protagoras, who was convicted because he had declared that he did not know whether the gods existed or not ; and as to such a process against Carneades, tradition would not have remained silent. Instead, we learn that he was employed as the trusted representative of the State on most important diplomatic missions. It is evident that Athens had arrived at the point of view that the theoretical denial of the gods might be tolerated, whereas the law, of course, continued to protect public worship.

In Rome they did not possess, as in Athens, a general statute against religious offences ; there were only special provisions, and they were, moreover, few and insufficient. This defect, however, was remedied by the vigorous police authority with which the Roman magistrates were invested. In Rome severe measures were often taken against movements which threatened the Roman official worship, but it was done at the discretion of the administration and not according to hard-and-fast rules ; hence the practice was somewhat varying, and a certain arbitrariness inevitable.

No example is known from Rome of action taken against theoretical denial of the gods corresponding to the trials of the philosophers in

Athens. The main cause of this was, no doubt, that free-thinking in the fifth century B.C. invaded Hellas, and specially Athens, like a flood which threatened to overthrow everything; in Rome, on the other hand, Greek philosophy made its way in slowly and gradually, and this took place at a time when in the country of its origin it had long ago found a *modus vivendi* with popular religion and was acknowledged as harmless to the established worship. The more practical outlook of the Romans may perhaps also have had something to say in the matter: they were rather indifferent to theoretical speculations, whereas they were not to be trifled with when their national institutions were concerned.

In consequence of this point of view the Roman government first came to deal with denial of the gods as a breach of law when confronted with the two monotheistic religions which invaded the Empire from the East. That which distinguished Jews and Christians from Pagans was not that they denied the existence of the Pagan gods—the Christians, at any rate, did not do this as a rule—but that they denied that they were gods, and therefore refused to worship them. They were practical, not theoretical deniers. The tolerance which the Roman government showed towards all foreign creeds and the result of which in imperial times was, practically speaking, freedom of religion over the whole Empire, could not be extended to the Jews and the Christians; for it was in the last resort based on reciprocity, on the fact that worship of the Egyptian or Persian gods did not exclude worship of the Roman ones. Every convert, on the other hand, won over to Judaism or Christianity was *eo ipso* an apostate from the Roman religion, an *atheos* according to the ancient conception. Hence, as soon as such religions began to spread, they constituted a serious danger to the established religion, and the Roman government intervened. Judaism and Christianity were not treated quite alike; in this connexion details are of no interest, but certain principal features must be dwelt on as significant of the attitude of antiquity towards denial of the gods. To simplify matters I confine myself to Christianity, where things are less complicated.

The Christians were generally designated as *atheoi*, as deniers of the gods, and the objection against them was precisely their denial of the Pagan gods, not their religion as such. When the Christian, summoned before the Roman magistrates, agreed to sacrifice to the Pagan gods (among them, the Emperor) he was acquitted; he was not punished for previously having attended Christian services, and it seems that he was not even required to undertake not to do so in future. Only if he refused to sacrifice, was he punished. We cannot ask for a clearer proof that it is apostasy as such, denial of the gods, against which action is taken. It is in keeping with this that, at any rate under the earlier Empire, no attempt was made to seek out the Christians at their assemblies, to hinder their services or the like; it was considered sufficient to take steps when information was laid.

The punishments meted out were different, in that they were left solely to the discretion of the magistrates. But they were generally severe : forced labour in mines and capital punishment were quite common. No discrimination was made between Roman citizens and others belonging to the Empire, but all were treated alike ; that the Roman citizen could not undergo capital punishment without appeal to the Emperor does not affect the principle. This procedure has really no expressly formulated basis in law ; the Roman penal code did not, as mentioned above, take cognizance of denial of the gods. Nevertheless, the sentences on the Christians were considered by the Pagans of the earlier time as a matter of course, the justice of which was not contested, and the procedure of the government was in principle the same under humane and conscientious rulers like Trajan and Marcus Aurelius as under tyrants like Nero and Domitian. Here again it is evident how firmly rooted in the mind of antiquity was the conviction that denial of the gods was a capital offence.

To resume what has here been set forth concerning the attitude of ancient society to atheism : it is, in the first place, evident that the frequently mentioned tolerance of polytheism was not extended to those who denied its gods ; in fact, it was applied only to those who acknowledged them even if they worshipped others besides. But the assertion of this principle of intolerance varied greatly in practice according to whether it was a question of theoretical denial of the gods—atheism in our sense—or practical refusal to worship the Pagan gods.   Against atheism the community took action only during a comparatively short period, and, as far as we know, only in a single place.   The latter limitation is probably explained not only by the defectiveness of tradition, but also by the fact that in Athens free-thinking made its appearance about the year 400 as a general phenomenon and therefore attracted the attention of the community.   Apart from this case, the philosophical denier of God was left in peace all through antiquity, in the same way as the individual citizen was not interfered with, as a rule, when he, for one reason or another, refrained from taking part in the worship of the deities.   On the other hand, as soon as practical refusal to believe in the gods, apostasy from the established religion, assumed dangerous proportions, ruthless severity was exercised against it.

The discrimination, however, made in the treatment of the theoretical and practical denial of the gods is certainly not due merely to consideration of the more or less isolated occurrence of the phenomenon ; it is rooted at the same time in the very nature of ancient religion.   The essence of ancient polytheism is the worship of the gods, that is, cultus ; of a doctrine of divinity properly speaking, of theology, there were only slight rudiments, and there was no idea of any elaborate dogmatic system. Quite different attitudes were accordingly assumed towards the philosopher, who held his own opinions of the gods, but took part in the public worship like anybody else ; and towards the monotheist, to whom the whole of the Pagan worship was an abomination, which one should abstain from at any cost, and which one should prevail on others to give up for the sake of their own good in this life or the next.

In the literature of antiquity we meet with sporadic statements to the effect that certain philosophers bore the epithet *atheos* as a sort of surname; and in a few of the later authors of antiquity we even find lists of men—almost all of them philosophers—who denied the existence of the gods. Furthermore, we possess information about certain persons—these also, if Jews and Christians are excluded, are nearly all of them philosophers—having been accused of, and eventually convicted of, denial of the gods; some of these are not in our lists. Information of this kind will, as remarked above, be taken as the point of departure for an investigation of atheism in antiquity. For practical reasons, however, it is reasonable to include some philosophers whom antiquity did not designate as atheists, and who did not come into conflict with official religion, but of whom it has been maintained in later times that they did not believe in the existence of the gods of popular belief. Thus we arrive at the following list, in which those who were denoted as *atheoi* are italicised and those who were accused of impiety are marked with an asterisk:

Xenophanes.
*Anaxagoras.
Diogenes of Apollonia.
Hippo of Rhegium.
*Protagoras.
Prodicus.
Critias.
Diagoras of Melos.
*Socrates.

Antisthenes.
Plato.
*Aristotle.
Theophrastus.
*Stilpo.
Theodorus.
Bion.
Epicurus.
Euhemerus.

The persons are put down in chronological order. This order will in some measure be preserved in the following survey; but regard for the continuity of the tradition of the doctrine will entail certain deviations. It will, that is to say, be natural to divide the material into four groups: the pre-Socratic philosophy; the Sophists; Socrates and the Socratics; Hellenistic philosophy. Each of these groups has a philosophical character of its own, and it will be seen that this character also makes itself felt in the relation to the gods of the popular belief, even though we here meet with phenomena of more isolated occurrence. The four groups must be supplemented by a fifth, a survey of the conditions in Imperial Rome. Atheists of this period are not found in our lists; but a good deal of old Pagan free-thinking survives in the first centuries of our era, and also the epithet *atheoi* was bestowed generally on the Christians and sometimes on the Jews, and if only for this reason they cannot be altogether passed by in this survey.

CHAPTER II

THE paganism of antiquity is based on a primitive religion, *i.e.* it is originally in the main homogeneous with the religions nowadays met with in the so-called primitive peoples. It underwent, however, a long process of evolution parallel with and conditioned by the development of Greek and later Roman civilisation. This evolution carried ancient religion far away from its primitive starting-point; it produced numerous new formations, above all a huge system of anthropomorphic gods, each with a definite character and personality of his own. This development is the result of an interplay of numerous factors: changing social and economical conditions evoked the desire for new religious ideas; the influence of other peoples made itself felt; poetry and the fine arts contributed largely to the moulding of these ideas; conscious reflection, too, arose early and modified original simplicity. But what is characteristic of the whole process is the fact that it went on continuously without breaks or sudden bounds. Nowhere in ancient religion, as far as we can trace it, did a powerful religious personality strike in with a radical transformation, with a direct rejection of old ideas and dogmatic accentuation of new ones. The result of this quiet growth was an exceedingly heterogeneous organism, in which remains of ancient, highly primitive customs and ideas were retained along with other elements of a far more advanced character.

Such a state of things need not in itself trouble the general consciousness ; it is a well-established fact that in religion the most divergent elements are not incompatible. Nevertheless, among the Greeks, with their strong proclivity to reflective thought, criticism early arose against the traditional conceptions of the gods. The typical method of this criticism is that the higher conceptions of the gods are used against the lower. From the earliest times the Greek religious sense favoured absoluteness of definition where the gods are concerned ; even in Homer they are not only eternal and happy, but also all-powerful and all-knowing. Corresponding expressions of a moral character are hardly to be found in Homer ; but as early as Hesiod and Solon we find, at any rate, Zeus as the representative of heavenly justice. With such definitions a large number of customs of public worship and, above all, a number of stories about the gods, were in violent contradiction ; thus we find even so old and so pious a poet as Pindar occasionally rejecting mythical stories which he thinks at variance with the sublime nature of the gods. This form of criticism of popular beliefs is continued through the whole of antiquity ; it is found not only in philosophers and philosophically educated laymen, but appears spontaneously in everybody of a reflective mind ; its best known representative in earlier times is Euripides. Typical of its popular form is in the first place its casualness; it is directed against details which at the moment attract attention, while it leaves other things alone which in principle are quite as offensive, but either not very obviously so, or else not relevant to the matter in hand. Secondly, it is naïve: it takes the gods of the popular belief for granted essentially as they are; it does not raise the crucial question whether the popular belief is not quite justified in attributing to these higher beings all kinds of imperfection, and wrong in attributing perfection to them, and still less if such beings, whether they are defined as perfect or imperfect, exist at all. It follows that as a whole this form of criticism is outside the scope of our inquiry.

Still, there is one single personality in early Greek thought who seems to have proceeded still further on the lines of this naïve criticism, namely, Xenophanes of Colophon. He is generally included amongst the philosophers, and rightly in so far as he initiated a philosophical speculation which was of the highest importance in the development of Greek scientific thought. But in the present connexion it would, nevertheless, be misleading to place Xenophanes among those philosophers who came into conflict with the popular belief because their conception of Existence was based on science. The starting-point for his criticism of the popular belief is in fact not philosophical, but religious; he ranks with personalities like Pindar and Euripides —he was also a verse-writer himself, with considerable poetic gift—and is only distinguished from them by the greater consistency of his thought. Hence, the correct course is to deal with him in this place as the only eminent thinker in antiquity about whom it is known that—starting from popular belief and religious motives—he reached a standpoint which at any rate with some truth may be designated as atheism.

Xenophanes lived in the latter part of the sixth and the beginning of the fifth centuries B.C. (according to his own statement he reached an age of more than ninety years). He was an itinerant singer who travelled about and recited poetry, presumably not merely his own but also that of others. In his own poems he severely attacked the manner in which Homer and Hesiod, the most famous poets of Greece, had represented the gods : they had attributed to them everything which in man's eyes is outrageous and reprehensible—theft, adultery and deception of one another. Their accounts of the fights of the gods against Titans and Giants he denounced as " inventions of the ancients." But he did not stop at that : " Men believe that the gods are born, are clothed and shaped and speak like themselves " ; " if oxen and horses and lions could draw and paint, they would delineate their gods in their own image " ; " the Negroes believe that their gods are flat-nosed and black, the Thracians that theirs have blue eyes and red hair." Thus he attacked directly the popular belief that the gods are anthropomorphic, and his arguments testify that he clearly realised that men create their gods in their own image. On another main point, too, he was in direct opposition to the religious ideas of his time : he rejected Divination, the belief that

the gods imparted the secrets of the future to men—
which was deemed a mainstay of the belief in the
existence of the gods. As a positive counterpart
to the anthropomorphic gods, Xenophanes set up
a philosophical conception of God: God must be
One, Eternal, Unchangeable and identical with
himself in every way (all sight, all hearing and all
mind). This deity, according to the explicit statements of our earliest sources, he identified with the
universe.

If we examine more closely the arguments put
forth by Xenophanes in support of his remarkable
conception of the deity, we realise that he everywhere starts from the definitions of the nature of
the gods as given by popular religion; but, be it
understood, solely from the absolute definitions.
He takes the existence of the divine, with its absolute
attributes, for granted; it is in fact the basis of all
his speculation. His criticism of the popular ideas
of the gods is therefore closely connected with his
philosophical conception of God; the two are the
positive and negative sides of the same thing.
Altogether his connexion with what I call the naïve
criticism of the popular religion is unmistakable.

It is undoubtedly a remarkable fact that we
meet at this early date with such a consistent
representative of this criticism. If we take Xenophanes at his word we must describe him as an
atheist, and atheism in the sixth century B.C. is a
very curious phenomenon indeed. Neither was it
acknowledged in antiquity; no one placed Xenophanes amongst *atheoi*; and Cicero even says
somewhere (according to Greek authority) that

Xenophanes was the only one of those who believed in gods who rejected divination.   In more recent times, too, serious doubt has been expressed whether Xenophanes actually denied the existence of the gods.   Reference has amongst other things been made to the fact that he speaks in several places about " gods " where he, according to his view, ought to say " God "; nay, he has even formulated his fundamental idea in the words : " One God, the greatest amongst gods and men, neither in shape nor mind like unto any mortal."   To be sure, Xeno- phanes is not always consistent in his language ; but no weight whatever ought to be attached to this, least of all in the case of a man who exclusively expressed himself in verse.   Another theory rests on the tradition that Xenophanes regarded his deity and the universe as identical, consequently was a pantheist.   In that case, it is said, he may very well have considered, for instance, the heavenly bodies as deities.   Sound as this argument is in general, it does not apply to this case.   When a thinker arrives at pantheism, starting from a criti- cism of polytheism which is expressly based on the antithesis between the unity and plurality of the deity—then very valid proofs, indeed, are needed in order to justify the assumption that he after all believed in a plurality of gods ; and such proofs are wanting in the case of Xenophanes.

Judging from the material in hand one can hardly arrive at any other conclusion than that the stand- point of Xenophanes comes under our definition of atheism.   But we must not forget that only frag- ments of his writings have been preserved, and that

the more extensive of them do not assist us greatly to the understanding of his religious standpoint. It is possible that we might have arrived at a different conclusion had we but possessed his chief philosophical work in its entirety, or at least larger portions of it. And I must candidly confess that if I were asked whether, in my heart of hearts, I believed that a Greek of the sixth century B.C. denied point-blank the existence of his gods, my answer would be in the negative.

That Xenophanes was not considered an atheist by the ancients may possibly be explained by the fact that they objected to fasten this designation on a man whose reasoning took the deity as a startingpoint and whose sole aim was to define its nature. Perhaps they also had an inkling that he in reality stood on the ground of popular belief, even if he went beyond it. Still more curious is the fact that his religious view does not seem to have influenced the immediately succeeding philosophy at all. His successors, Parmenides and Zeno, developed his doctrine of unity, but in a pantheistic direction, and on a logical, not religious line of argument ; about their attitude to popular belief we are told practically nothing. And Ionic speculation took a quite different direction. Not till a century later, in Euripides, do we observe a distinct influence of his criticism of popular belief ; but at that time other currents of opinion had intervened which are not dependent on Xenophanes, but might direct attention to him.

3

CHAPTER III

ANCIENT Greek naturalism is essentially calculated to collide with the popular belief. It seeks a natural explanation of the world, first and foremost of its origin, but in the next place of individual natural phenomena. As to the genesis of the world, speculations of a mythical kind had already developed on the basis of the popular belief. They were not, however, binding on anybody, and, above all, the idea of the gods having created the world was altogether alien to Greek religion. Thus, without offence to them it might be maintained that everything originated from a primary substance or from a mixture of several primary substances, as was generally maintained by the ancient naturalists. On the other hand, a conflict arose as soon as the heavenly phenomena, such as lightning and thunder, were ascribed to natural causes, or when the heavenly bodies were made out to be natural objects ; for to the Greeks it was an established fact that Zeus sent lightning and thunder, and that the sun and the moon were gods. A refusal to believe in the latter was especially dangerous because they were *visible* gods, and as to the person who did not believe in their divinity the obvious conclusion would be that he believed still less in the invisible gods.

That this inference was drawn will appear before long. But the epithet " atheist " was very rarely attached to the ancient naturalists ; only a few of the later (and those the least important) were given the nickname *atheos*. Altogether we hear very little of the relation of these philosophers to the popular belief, and this very silence is surely significant. No doubt, most of them bestowed but a scant attention on this aspect of the matter ; they were engrossed in speculations which did not bring them into conflict with the popular belief, and even their scientific treatment of the " divine " natural phenomena did not make them doubt the *existence* of the gods. This is connected with a peculiarity in their conception of existence. Tradition tells us of several of them, and it applies presumably also to those of whom it is not recorded, that they designated their primary substance or substances as gods ; sometimes they also applied this designation to the world or worlds originating in the primary substance. This view is deeply rooted in the Greek popular belief and harmonises with its fundamental view of existence. To these ancient thinkers the primary substance is at once a living and a super-human power ; and any living power which transcended that of man was divine to the Greeks. Hylozoism (the theory that matter is alive) consequently, when it allies itself with popular belief, leads straight to pantheism, whereas it excludes monotheism, which presupposes a distinction between god and matter. Now it is a matter of experience that, while monotheism is the hereditary foe of polytheism, polytheism and pantheism go

very well together. The universe being divine,
there is no reason to doubt that beings of a higher
order than man exist, nor any reason to refuse to
bestow on them the predicate " divine " ; and with
this we find ourselves in principle on the standpoint
of polytheistic popular belief. There is nothing
surprising, then, in the tradition that Thales
identified God with the mind of the universe and
believed the universe to be animated, and filled with
" demons." The first statement is in this form
probably influenced by later ideas and hardly a
correct expression of the view of Thales ; the rest
bears the very stamp of genuineness, and similar
ideas recur, more or less completely and variously
refracted, in the succeeding philosophers.

To follow these variations in detail is outside the
scope of this investigation ; but it may be of interest
to see the form they take in one of the latest and
most advanced representatives of Ionian naturalism.
In Democritus's conception of the universe, personal
gods would seem excluded *a priori*. He works with
but three premises : the atoms, their movements,
and empty space. From this everything is derived
according to strict causality. Such phenomena
also as thunder and lightning, comets and eclipses,
which were generally ascribed to the gods, are
according to his opinion due to natural causes,
whereas people in the olden days were afraid of them
because they believed they were due to the gods.
Nevertheless, he seems, in the first place, to have
designated Fire, which he at the same time recognised as a " soul-substance," as divine, the cosmic
fire being the soul of the world; and secondly,

he thought that there was something real underlying the popular conception of the gods. He was led to this from a consideration of dreams, which he thought were images of real objects which entered into the sleeper through the pores of the body. Now, since gods might be seen in dreams, they must be real beings. He did actually say that the gods had more senses than the ordinary five. When he who of all the Greek philosophers went furthest in a purely mechanical conception of nature took up such an attitude to the religion of his people, one cannot expect the others, who were less advanced, to discard it.

Nevertheless, there is a certain probability that some of the later Ionian naturalists went further in their criticism of the gods of popular belief. One of them actually came into conflict with popular religion ; it will be natural to begin with him.

Shortly before the outbreak of the Peloponnesian War, Anaxagoras of Clazomenae was accused of impiety and had to leave Athens, where he had taken up his abode. The object of the accusation was in reality political ; the idea being to hit Pericles through his friend the naturalist. What Anaxagoras was charged with was that he had assumed that the heavenly bodies were natural objects ; he had taught that the sun was a red-hot mass, and that the moon was earth and larger than Peloponnese. To base an accusation of impiety on this, it was necessary first to carry a public resolution, giving power to prosecute those who gave natural explanations of heavenly phenomena.

As to Anaxagoras's attitude to popular belief, we hear next to nothing apart from this. There is a story of a ram's head being found with one horn in the middle of the forehead; it was brought to Pericles, and the soothsayer Lampon explained the portent to the effect that, of the two men, Pericles and Thucydides, who contended for the leadership of Athens, one should prove victorious. Anaxagoras, on the other hand, had the ram's head cut open and showed that the brain did not fill up the cranium, but was egg-shaped and lay gathered together at the point where the horn grew out. He evidently thought that abortions also, which otherwise were generally considered as signs from the gods, were due to natural causes. Beyond this, nothing is said of any attack on the popular belief on the part of Anaxagoras, and in his philosophy nothing occurred which logically entailed a denial of the existence of the gods. Add to this that it was necessary to create a new judicial basis for the accusation against Anaxagoras, and it can be taken as certain that neither in his writings nor in any other way did he come forward in public as a denier of the gods.

It is somewhat different when we consider the purely personal point of view of Anaxagoras. The very fact that no expression of his opinion concerning the gods has been transmitted affords food for thought. Presumably there was none; but this very fact is notable when we bear in mind that the earlier naturalists show no such reticence. Add to this that, if there is any place and any time in which we might expect a complete emancipation

from popular belief, combined with a decided dis-
inclination to give expression to it, it is Athens
under Pericles. Men like Pericles and his friends
represent a high level, perhaps the zenith, in Hellenic
culture. That they were critical of many of the
religious conceptions of their time we may take for
granted ; as to Pericles himself, this is actually
stated as a fact, and the accusations of impiety
directed against Aspasia and Pheidias prove that
orthodox circles were very well aware of it.
But the accusations prove, moreover, that Pericles
and those who shared his views were so much in
advance of their time that they could not afford
to let their free-thinking attitude become a matter
of public knowledge without endangering their
political position certainly, and possibly even more
than that. To be sure, considerations of that kind
did not weigh with Anaxagoras ; but he was—and
that we know on good authority—a quiet scholar
whose ideal of life was to devote himself to problems
of natural science, and he can hardly have wished
to be disturbed in this occupation by affairs in which
he took no sort of interest. The question is then
only how far men like Pericles and himself may have
ventured in their criticism. Though all direct
tradition is wanting, we have at any rate circumstantial evidence possessing a certain degree of
probability.

To begin with, the attempt to give a natural
explanation of prodigies is not in itself without
interest. The mantic art, *i.e.* the ability to predict
the future by signs from the gods or direct divine
inspiration, was throughout antiquity considered

one of the surest proofs of the existence of the gods. Now, it by no means follows that a person who was not impressed by a deformed ram's head would deny, *e.g.*, the ability of the Delphic Oracle to predict the future, especially not so when the person in question was a naturalist. But that there was at this time a general tendency to reject the art of divination is evident from the fact that Herodotus as well as Sophocles, both of them contemporaries of Pericles and Anaxagoras, expressly contend against attempts in that direction, and, be it remarked, as if the theory they attack was commonly held. Sophocles is in this connexion so far the more interesting of the two, as, on one hand, he criticises private divination but defends the Delphic oracle vigorously, while he, on the other hand, identifies denial of the oracle with denial of the gods. And he does this in such a way as to make it evident that he has a definite object in mind. That in this polemic he may have been aiming precisely at Anaxagoras is indicated by the fact that Diopeithes, who carried the resolution concerning the accusation of the philosopher, was a soothsayer by profession.

The strongest evidence as to the free-thinking of the Periclean age is, however, to be met with in the historical writing of Thucydides. In his work on the Peloponnesian War, Thucydides completely eliminated the supernatural element ; not only did he throughout ignore omens and divinations, except in so far as they played a part as a psychological factor, but he also completely omitted any reference to the gods in his narrative. Such a procedure was at this time unprecedented, and contrasts sharply with that of his immediate forerunner Herodotus, who constantly lays stress on the intervention of the gods. That is hardly conceivable except in a man who had altogether emancipated himself from the religious views of his time. Now, Thucydides is not only a fellow-countryman and younger contemporary of Pericles, but he also sees in Pericles his ideal not only as a politician but evidently also as a man. Hence, when everything is considered, it is not improbable that Pericles and his friends went to all lengths in their criticism of popular belief, although, of course, it remains impossible to state anything definite as to particular persons' individual views. Curiously enough, even in antiquity this connexion was observed ; in a biography of Thucydides it is said that he was a disciple of Anaxagoras and *accordingly* was also considered something of an atheist.

While Anaxagoras, his trial notwithstanding, is not generally designated an atheist, probably because there was nothing in his writings to which he might be pinned down, that fate befel two of his contemporaries, Hippo of Rhegium and Diogenes of Apollonia. Very little, however, is known of them. Hippo, who is said to have been a Pythagorean, taught that water and fire were the origin of everything ; as to the reason why he earned the nickname *atheos*, it is said that he taught that Water was the primal cause of all, as well as that he maintained that nothing existed but what could be perceived by the senses. There is also quoted a (fictitious) inscription, which he is said to have caused to be put on his tomb, to the effect that Death has made him the equal of the immortal gods (in that he now exists no more than they).   Otherwise we know nothing special of Hippo ; Aristotle refers to him as shallow. As to Diogenes, we learn that he was influenced by Anaximenes and Anaxagoras ; in agreement with the former he regarded Air as the primary substance, and like Anaxagoras he attributed reason to his primary substance.   Of his doctrine we have extensive accounts, and also some not inconsiderable fragments of his treatise *On Nature* ; but they are almost all of them of purely scientific, mostly of an anatomical and physiological character. In especial, as to his relation to popular belief, it is recorded that he identified Zeus with the air.   Indirectly, however, we are able to demonstrate, by the aid of an almost contemporary witness, that there must have been some foundation for the accusation of " atheism."   For in *The Clouds*, where Aristophanes wants to represent Socrates as an atheist, he puts in his mouth scraps of the naturalism of Diogenes ; that he would hardly have done, if Diogenes had not already been decried as an atheist.

It is of course impossible to base any statement of the relation of the two philosophers to popular belief on such a foundation.   But it is, nevertheless, worth noticing that while not a single one of the earlier naturalists acquired the designation atheist, it was applied to two of the latest and otherwise little-known representatives of the school.   Take this in combination with what has been said above of Anaxagoras, and we get at any rate a suspicion that Greek naturalism gradually led its adherents beyond the naïve stage where many individual phenomena were indeed ascribed to natural causes, even if they had formerly been regarded as caused by divine intervention, but where the foundations of the popular belief were left untouched. Once this path has been entered on, a point will be arrived at where the final conclusion is drawn and the existence of the supernatural completely denied. It is probable that this happened towards the close of the naturalistic period. If so early a philosopher as Anaxagoras took this point of view, his personal contribution as a member of the Periclean circle may have been more significant in the religious field than one would conjecture from the character of his work.

Before we proceed to mention the sophists, there is one person on our list who must be examined though the result will be negative, namely, Diagoras of Melos. As he appears in our records, he falls outside the classification adopted here ; but as he must have lived, at any rate, about the middle of the fifth century (he is said to have " flourished " in 464) he may most fitly be placed on the boundary line between the Ionian philosophy and Sophistic.

For later antiquity Diagoras is the typical atheist ; he heads our lists of atheists, and round his person a whole series of myths have been formed. He is said to have been a poet and a pious man like others ; but then a colleague once stole an ode from him, escaped by taking an oath that he was innocent, and afterwards made a hit with the stolen work.

So Diagoras lost his faith in the gods and wrote a treatise under the title of *apopyrgizontes logoi* (literally, destructive considerations) in which he attacked the belief in the gods.

This looks very plausible, and is interesting in so far as it, if correct, affords an instance of atheism arising in a layman from actual experience, not in a philosopher from speculation. If we ask, however, what is known historically about Diagoras, we are told a different tale. There existed in Athens, engraved on a bronze tablet and set up on the Acropolis, a decree of the people offering a reward of one talent to him who should kill Diagoras of Melos, and of two talents to him who should bring him alive to Athens. The reason given was that he had scoffed at the Eleusinian Mysteries and divulged what took place at them. The date of this decree is given by a historian as 415 B.C.; that this is correct is seen from a passage in Aristophanes's contemporary drama, *The Birds*. Furthermore, one of the disciples of Aristotle, the literary historian Aristoxenus, states that no trace of impiety was to be found in the works of the dithyrambic poet Diagoras, and that, in fact, they contained definite opinions to the contrary. A remark to the effect that Diagoras was instrumental in drawing up the laws of Mantinea is probably due to the same source. The context shows that the reference is to the earlier constitution of Mantinea, which was a mixture of aristocracy and democracy, and is praised for its excellence. It is inconceivable that, in a Peloponnesian city during the course of, nay, presumably even before the middle of the fifth century, a notorious atheist should have been invited to advise on the revision of its constitution.   It is more probable that Aristoxenus adduced this fact as an additional disproof of Diagoras's atheism, in which he evidently did not believe.

The above information explains the origin of the legend.   Two fixed points were in existence : the pious poet of *c.* 460 and the atheist who was outlawed in 415 ; a bridge was constructed between them by the story of the stolen ode.   This disposes of the whole supposition of atheism growing out of a basis of experience.   But, furthermore, it must be admitted that it is doubtful whether the poet and the atheist are one and the same person.   The interval of time between them is itself suspicious, for the poet, according to the ancient system of calculation, must have been about forty years old in 464, consequently between eighty and ninety in 415.   (There is general agreement that the treatise, the title of which has been quoted, must have been a later forgery.)   If, in spite of all, I dare not absolutely deny the identity of the two Diagorases of tradition, the reason is that Aristophanes, where he mentions the decree concerning Diagoras, seems to suggest that his attack on the Mysteries was an old story which was raked up again in 415.   But for our purpose, at any rate, nothing remains of the copious mass of legend but the fact that one Diagoras of Melos in 415 was outlawed in Athens on the ground of his attack on the Mysteries.   Such an attack may have been the outcome of atheism ; there was no lack of impiety in Athens at the end

of the fifth century.   But whether this was the case
or not we cannot possibly tell ; and to throw light
on free-thinking tendencies in Athens at this time,
we have other and richer sources than the historical
notice of Diagoras.

CHAPTER IV

WITH the movement in Greek thought which is generally known as sophistic, a new view of popular belief appears. The criticism of the sophists was directed against the entire tradition on which Greek society was based, and principally against the moral conceptions which hitherto had been unquestioned : good and evil, right and wrong. The criticism was essentially negative ; that which hitherto had been imagined as absolute was demonstrated to be relative, and the relative was identified with the invalid. Thus they could not help running up against the popular ideas of the gods, and treating them in the same way. A leading part was here played by the sophistic distinction between *nomos* and *physis*, Law and Nature, *i.e.* that which is based on human convention, and that which is founded on the nature of things. The sophists could not help seeing that the whole public worship and the ideas associated with it belonged to the former—to the domain of " the law." Not only did the worship and the conceptions of the gods vary from place to place in the hundreds of small independent communities into which Hellas was divided—a fact which the sophists had special opportunity of observing when travelling from town to town to teach ; but it was even officially admitted that the whole ritual—which, popularly speaking, was almost identical with religion—was based on convention. If a Greek was asked why a god was to be worshipped in such and such a way, generally the only answer was : because it is the law of the State (or the convention ; the word *nomos* expresses both things). Hence it followed in principle that religion came under the domain of " the law," being consequently the work of man ; and hence again the obvious conclusion, according to sophistic reasoning, was that it was nothing but human imagination, and that there was no *physis*, no reality, behind it at all. In the case of the naturalists, it was the positive foundation of their system, their conception of nature as a whole, that led them to criticise the popular belief. Hence their criticism was in the main only directed against those particular ideas in the popular belief which were at variance with the results of their investigations. To be sure, the sophists were not above making use of the results of natural science in their criticism of the popular belief ; it was their general aim to impart the highest education of their time, and of a liberal education natural science formed a rather important part. But their starting-point was quite different from that of the naturalists. Their whole interest was concentrated on man as a member of the community, and it was from consideration of this relation that they were brought into collision with the established religion. Hence their attack was far more dangerous than that of the naturalists ; no longer was it directed against details, it laid bare the psychological basis itself of popular belief and clearly revealed its unstable character. Their criticism was fundamental and central, not casual and circumstantial.

From a purely practical point of view also, the criticism of the sophists was far more dangerous than that of the old philosophers. They were not theorists themselves, but practitioners ; their business was to impart the higher education to the more mature youth. It was therefore part of their profession to disseminate their views not by means of learned professional writings, but by the persuasive eloquence of oral discourse. And in their criticism of the existing state of things they did not start with special results which only science could prove, and the correctness of which the layman need not recognise ; they operated with facts and principles known and acknowledged by everybody. It is not to be wondered at that such efforts evoked a vigorous reaction on the part of established society, the more so as in any case the result of sophistic criticism—though not consciously its object—was to liquefy the moral principles on which the social order was based.

Such, in principle, appeared to be the state of things. In practice, here as elsewhere, the devil proved not so black as he was painted. First, not all the sophists—hardly even the majority of them —drew the logical conclusions from their views in respect of either morals or religion. They were teachers of rhetoric, and as such they taught, for instance, all the tricks by which a bad cause might be defended ; that was part of the trade. But it must be supposed that Gorgias, the most distinguished of them, expressly insisted that rhetoric, just like any other art the aim of which was to defeat an opponent, should only be used for good ends. Similarly many of them may have stopped short in their criticism of popular belief at some arbitrary point, so that it was possible for them to respect at any rate something of the established religion, and so, of course, first and foremost the very belief in the existence of the gods. That they did not as a rule interfere with public worship, we may be sure ; that was based firmly on " the Law." But, in addition, even sophists who personally took an attitude radically contradictory to popular belief had the most important reasons for being careful in advancing such a view. They had to live by being the teachers of youth ; they had no fixed appointment, they travelled about as lecturers and enlisted disciples by means of their lectures. For such men it would have been a very serious thing to attack the established order in its tenderest place, religion, and above all they had to beware of coming into conflict with the penal laws. This risk they did not incur while confining themselves to theoretical discussions about right and wrong, nor by the practical application of them in their teaching of rhetoric ; but they might very easily incur it if attacking religion.

This being the case, it is not to be wondered at that we do not find many direct statements of undoubtedly atheistical character handed down from the more eminent sophists, and that trials for impiety are rare in their case. But, nevertheless, a few such cases are met with, and from these as our starting-point we will now proceed.

As to Protagoras of Abdera, one of the earliest and most famous of all the sophists, it is stated that he began a pamphlet treating of the gods with the words : " Concerning the gods I can say nothing, neither that they exist nor that they do not exist, nor of what form they are ; because there are many things which prevent one from knowing that, namely, both the uncertainty of the matter and the shortness of man's life." On this account, it is said, he was charged with impiety at Athens and was outlawed, and his works were publicly burned. The date of this trial is not known for certain ; but it is reasonably supposed to have coincided with that of Diagoras, namely, in 415. At any rate it must have taken place after 423–421, as we know that Protagoras was at that time staying in Athens. As he must have been born about 485, the charge overtook him when old and famous ; according to one account, his work on the gods seems to belong to his earlier writings.

To doubt the correctness of this tradition would require stronger reasons than we possess, although it is rather strange that the condemnation of Protagoras is mentioned neither in our historical sources nor in Aristophanes, and that Plato, who mentions Protagoras rather frequently as dead, never alludes to it. At any rate, the quotation from the work on the gods is certainly authentic, for Plato himself referred to it. Hence it is certain that Protagoras directly stated the problem as to the existence of the gods and regarded it as an open question. But beyond that nothing much can be deduced from the short quotation ; and as to the rest of the book on the gods we know nothing. The meagre reasons for scepticism adduced probably do not imply any more than that the difficulties are objective as well as subjective. If, in the latter respect, the brevity of life is specially mentioned it may be supposed that Protagoras had in mind a definite proof of the existence of the gods which was rendered difficult by the fact that life is so brief; prediction of the future may be guessed at, but nothing certain can be stated.

Protagoras is the only one of the sophists of whom tradition says that he was the object of persecution owing to his religious views. The trial of Socrates, however, really belongs to the same category when looked at from the accusers' point of view; Socrates was accused as a sophist. But as his own attitude towards popular religion differed essentially from that of the sophists, we cannot consider him in this connexion. Protagoras's trial itself is partly determined by special circumstances. In all probability it took place at a moment when a violent religious reaction had set in at Athens owing to some grave offences against the public worship and sanctuaries of the State (violation of the Mysteries and mutilation of the Hermae). The work on the gods had presumably been in existence and known long before this without causing scandal to anybody. But, nevertheless, the trial, like those of Anaxagoras and Socrates, plainly bears witness to the animosity with which the modern freethought was regarded in Athens. This animosity did not easily manifest itself publicly without special reasons; but it was always there and might always be used in case of provocation.

As to Protagoras's personal attitude to the question of the existence of the gods, much may be guessed and much has been guessed; but nothing can be stated for certain. However, judging from the man's profession and his general habit of life as it appears in tradition, we may take for granted that he did not give offence in his outward behaviour by taking a hostile attitude to public worship or attacking its foundations; had that been so, he would not for forty years have been the most distinguished teacher of Hellas, but would simply not have been tolerated. An eminent modern scholar has therefore advanced the conjecture that Protagoras distinguished between belief and knowledge, and that his work on the gods only aimed at showing that the existence of the gods could not be scientifically demonstrated. Now such a distinction probably, if conceived as a conscious principle, is alien to ancient thought, at any rate at the time of Protagoras; and yet it may contain a grain of truth. When it is borne in mind that the incriminated passage represents the very exordium of the work of Protagoras, the impression cannot be avoided that he himself did not intend his work to disturb the established religion, but that he quite naïvely took up the existence of the gods as a subject, as good as any other, for dialectic discussion. All that he was concerned with was theory and theorising; religion was practice and ritual; and he had no more intention of interfering with that than the other earlier sophists of assailing the legal system of the community in their speculation as to relativity of right and wrong.

All this, however, does not alter the fact that the work of Protagoras posed the very question of the existence of the gods as a problem which might possibly be solved in the negative. He seems to have been the first to do this. That it could be done is significant of the age to which Protagoras belongs; that it was done was undoubtedly of great importance for the development of thought in wide circles.

Prodicus of Ceos, also one of the most famous sophists, advanced the idea that the conceptions of the gods were originally associated with those things which were of use to humanity: sun and moon, rivers and springs, the products of the earth and the elements; therefore bread was identified with Demeter, wine with Dionysus, water with Poseidon, fire with Hephaestus. As a special instance he mentioned the worship of the Nile by the Egyptians.

In Democritus, who was a slightly elder contemporary of Prodicus, we have already met with investigation into the origin of the conceptions of the gods. There is a close parallel between his handling of the subject and that of Prodicus, but at the same time a characteristic difference. Democritus was a naturalist, hence he took as his starting-point the natural phenomena commonly ascribed to the influence of the gods. Prodicus, on the other hand, started from the intellectual life of man. We learn that he had commenced to study synonyms, and that he was interested in the interpretation of

the poets.   Now he found that Homer occasionally
simply substituted the name of Hephaestus for fire,
and that other poets went even further on the same
lines.   Furthermore, while it was common knowledge to every Greek that certain natural objects,
such as the heavenly bodies and the rivers, were
regarded as divine and had names in common with
their gods, this to Prodicus would be a specially
attractive subject for speculation.   It is plainly
shown by his instances that it is linguistic observations of this kind which were the starting-point of
his theory concerning the origin of the conceptions
of the gods.

In the accounts of Prodicus it is taken for granted
that he denied the existence of the gods, and in
later times he is classed as *atheos*.   Nevertheless
we have every reason to doubt the correctness of
this opinion.   The case of Democritus already shows
that a philosopher might very well derive the conceptions of the gods from an incorrect interpretation
of certain phenomena without throwing doubt on
their existence.   As far as Prodicus is concerned it
may be assumed that he did not believe that Bread,
Wine or Fire were gods, any more than Democritus
imagined that Zeus sent thunder and lightning ;
nor, presumably, did he ever believe that rivers
were gods.   But he need not therefore have denied
the existence of Demeter, Dionysus and Hephaestus,
much less the divinity of the sun and the moon.
And if we consider his theory more closely it points
in quite a different direction from that of atheism.
To Prodicus it was evidently the conception of
utility that mattered : if these objects came to be

regarded as gods it was because they " benefited humanity." This too is a genuinely sophistic view, characteristically deviating from that of the naturalist Democritus in its limitation to the human and social aspect of the question. Such a point of view, if confronted with the question of the existence of the gods, may very well, according to sophistic methods of reasoning, lead to the conclusion that primitive man was right in so far as the useful, *i.e.* that which " benefits humanity," really is an essential feature of the gods, and wrong only in so far as he identified the individual useful objects with the gods. Whether Prodicus adopted this point of view, we cannot possibly tell ; but the general body of tradition concerning the man, which does not in any way suggest religious radicalism, indicates as most probable that he did not connect the question of the origin of the conceptions of the gods with that of the existence of the gods, which to him was taken for granted, and that it was only later philosophers who, in their researches into the ideas of earlier philosophers about the gods, inferred his atheism from his speculations on the history of religion.

Critias, the well-known reactionary politician, the chief of the Thirty Tyrants, is placed amongst the atheists on the strength of a passage in a satyric drama, *Sisyphus*. The drama is lost, but our authority quotes the objectionable passage *in extenso* ; it is a piece of no less than forty lines. The passage argues that human life in its origins knew no social order, that might ruled supreme. Then men conceived the idea of making laws in order that right might rule instead of might. The result of this was, it is true, that wrong was not done openly ; but it was done secretly instead. Then a wise man bethought himself of making men believe that there existed gods who saw and heard every-thing which men did, nay even knew their inner-most thoughts. And, in order that men might stand in proper awe of the gods, he said that they lived in the sky, out of which comes that which makes men afraid, such as lightning and thunder, but also that which benefits them, sunshine and rain, and the stars, those fair ornaments by whose course men measure time. Thus he succeeded in bringing law-lessness to an end. It is expressly stated that it was all a cunning fraud : " by such talk he made his teaching most acceptable, veiling truth with false words."

In antiquity it was disputed whether the drama *Sisyphus* was by Critias or Euripides ; nowadays all agree in attributing it to Critias ; nor does the style of the long fragment resemble that of Euripides. The question is, however, of no consequence in this connexion : whether the drama is by Critias or Euripides it is wrong to attribute to an author opinions which he has put into the mouth of a char-acter in a drama. Moreover, *Sisyphus* was a satyric play, *i.e.* it belonged to a class of poetry the liberty of which was nearly as great as in comedy, and the speech was delivered by Sisyphus himself, who, according to the legend, is a type of the crafty criminal whose forte is to do evil and elude punish-ment. There is, in fact, nothing in that which we otherwise hear of Critias to suggest that he cherished

free-thinking views.   He was—or in his later years
became—a fanatical adversary of the Attic democracy, and he was, when he held power, unscrupulous
in his choice of the means with which he opposed
it and the men who stood in the path of his reactionary policy ; but in our earlier sources he is never
accused of impiety in the theoretical sense.   And
yet there had been an excellent opportunity of
bringing forward such an accusation ; for in his
youth Critias had been a companion of Socrates,
and his later conduct was used as a proof that
Socrates corrupted his surroundings.   But it is
always Critias's political crimes which are adduced
in this connexion, not his irreligion.   On the other
hand, posterity looked upon him as the pure type of
tyrant, and the label atheist therefore suggested
itself on the slightest provocation.

But, even if the *Sisyphus* fragment cannot be
used to characterise its author as an atheist, it is,
nevertheless, of the greatest interest in this connexion, and therefore demands closer analysis.

The introductory idea, that mankind has
evolved from an animal state into higher stages,
is at variance with the earlier Greek conception,
namely, that history begins with a golden age
from which there is a continual decline.   The theory
of the fragment is expressed by a series of authors
from the same and the immediately succeeding
period.   It occurs in Euripides ; a later and otherwise little-known tragedian, Moschion, developed
it in detail in a still extant fragment ; Plato
accepted it and made it the basis of his presentation
of the origin of the State ; Aristotle takes it for

granted. Its source, too, has been demonstrated : it was presumably Democritus who first advanced it. Nevertheless the author of the fragment has hardly got it direct from Democritus, who at this time was little known at Athens, but from an intermediary. This intermediary is probably Protagoras, of whom it is said that he composed a treatise, *The Original State, i.e.* the primary state of mankind. Protagoras was a fellow-townsman of Democritus, and recorded by tradition as one of his direct disciples.

In another point also the fragment seems to betray the influence of Democritus. When it is said that the wise inventors of the gods made them dwell in the skies, because from the skies come those natural phenomena which frighten men, it is highly suggestive of Democritus's criticism of the divine explanation of thunder and lightning and the like. In this case also Protagoras may have been the intermediary. In his work on the gods he had every opportunity of discussing the question in detail. But here we have the theory of Democritus combined with that of Prodicus in that it is maintained that from the skies come also those things that benefit men, and that they are on this account also a suitable dwelling-place for the gods. It is obvious that the author of the fragment (or his source) was versed in the most modern wisdom.

All this erudition, however, is made to serve a certain tendency : the well-known tendency to represent religion as a political invention having as its object the policing of society. It is a theory which in antiquity—to its honour be it said—is but

of rare occurrence.   There is a vague indication of
it in Euripides, a more definite one in Aristotle, and
an elaborate application of it in Polybius ; and that
is in reality all.   (That many people in more enlightened ages upheld religion as a means of keeping
the masses in check, is a different matter.)   However, it is an interesting fact that the Critias fragment is not only the first evidence of the existence
of the theory known to us, but also presumably the
earliest and probably the best known to later antiquity.   Otherwise we should not find reference for
the theory made to a fragment of a farce, but to a
quotation from a philosopher.

This might lead us to conclude that the theory
was Critias's own invention, though, of course, it
would not follow that he himself adhered to it.
But it is more probable that it was a ready-made
modern theory which Critias put into the mouth
of Sisyphus.   Not only does the whole character
of the fragment and its scene of action favour this
supposition, but there is also another factor which
corroborates it.

In the *Gorgias* Plato makes one of the characters,
Callicles—a man of whom we otherwise know
nothing—profess a doctrine which up to a certain
point is almost identical with that of the fragment.
According to Callicles, the natural state (and the
right state ; on this point he is at variance with the
fragment) is that right belongs to the strong.   This
state has been corrupted by legislation ; the laws
are inventions of the weak, who are also the majority,
and their aim is to hinder the encroachment of the
strong.   If this theory is carried to its conclusion,

it is obvious that religion must be added to the laws; if the former is not also regarded as an invention for the policing of society, the whole theory is upset. Now in the *Gorgias* the question as to the attitude of the gods towards the problem of what is right and what is wrong is carefully avoided in the discussion. Not till the close of the dialogue, where Plato substitutes myth for scientific research, does he draw the conclusion in respect of religion. He does this in a positive form, as a consequence of *his* point of view: after death the gods reward the just and punish the unjust; but he expressly assumes that Callicles will regard it all as an old wives' tale.

In Callicles an attempt has been made to see a pseudonym for Critias. That is certainly wrong. Critias was a kinsman of Plato, is introduced by name in several dialogues, nay, one dialogue even bears his name, and he is everywhere treated with respect and sympathy. Nowadays, therefore, it is generally acknowledged that Callicles is a real person, merely unknown to us as such. However that may be, Plato would never have let a leading character in one of his longer dialogues advance (and Socrates refute) a view which had no better authority than a passage in a satyric drama. On the other hand, there is, as shown above, difficulty in supposing that the doctrine of the fragment was stated in the writings of an eminent sophist; so we come to the conclusion that it was developed and diffused in sophistic circles by oral teaching, and that it became known to Critias and Plato in this way. Its originator we do not know. We might

think of the sophist Thrasymachus, who in the first
book of Plato's *Republic* maintains a point of view
corresponding to that of Callicles in *Gorgias*.   But
what we otherwise learn of Thrasymachus is not
suggestive of interest in religion, and the only statement of his as to that kind of thing which has come
down to us tends to the denial of a providence, not
denial of the gods.   Quite recently Diagoras of
Melos has been guessed at ; this is empty talk,
resulting at best in substituting x (or NN) for y.

If I have dwelt in such detail on the *Sisyphus*
fragment, it is because it is our first direct and
unmistakable evidence of ancient atheism.   Here
for the first time we meet with the direct statement
which we have searched for in vain among all the
preceding authors : that the gods of popular belief
are fabrication pure and simple and without any
corresponding reality, however remote.   The nature
of our tradition precludes our ascertaining whether
such a statement might have been made earlier ;
but the probability is *a priori* that it was not.   The
whole development of ancient reasoning on religious
questions, as far as we are able to survey it, leads in
reality to the conclusion that atheism as an expressed
(though perhaps not publicly expressed) confession
of faith did not appear till the age of the sophists.

With the Critias fragment we have also brought
to an end the inquiry into the direct statements of
atheistic tendency which have come down to us
from the age of the sophists.   The result is, as we see,
rather meagre.   But it may be supplemented with
indirect testimonies which prove that there was
more of the thing than the direct tradition would

lead us to conjecture, and that the denial of the existence of the gods must have penetrated very wide circles.

The fullest expression of Attic free-thought at the end of the fifth century is to be found in the tragedies of Euripides. They are leavened with reflections on all possible moral and religious problems, and criticism of the traditional conceptions of the gods plays a leading part in them. We shall, however, have some difficulty in using Euripides as a source of what people really thought at this period, partly because he is a very pronounced personality and by no means a mere mouthpiece for the ideas of his contemporaries—during his lifetime he was an object of the most violent animosity owing, among other things, to his free-thinking views— partly because he, as a dramatist, was obliged to put his ideas into the mouths of his characters, so that in many cases it is difficult to decide how much is due to dramatic considerations and how much to the personal opinion of the poet. Even to this day the religious standpoint of Euripides is matter of dispute. In the most recent detailed treatment of the question he is characterised as an atheist, whereas others regard him merely as a dialectician who debates problems without having any real standpoint of his own.

I do not believe that Euripides personally denied the existence of the gods ; there is too much that tells against that theory, and, in fact, nothing that tells directly in favour of it, though he did not quite escape the charge of atheism even in his own day. To prove the correctness of this view would, however,

lead too far afield in this connexion.   On the other
hand, a short characterisation of Euripides's manner
of reasoning about religious problems is unavoidable
as a background for the treatment of those—very
rare—passages where he has put actually atheistic
reflections into the mouths of his characters.

As a Greek dramatist Euripides had to derive his
subjects from the heroic legends, which at the same
time were legends of the gods in so far as they were
interwoven with tales of the gods' direct intervention
in affairs.   It is precisely against this intervention
that the criticism of Euripides is primarily directed.
Again and again he makes his characters protest
against the manner in which they are treated by
the gods or in which the gods generally behave.
It is characteristic of Euripides that his starting-
point in this connexion is always the moral one.
So far he is a typical representative of that tendency
which, in earlier times, was represented by Xenophanes and a little later by Pindar ; in no other
Greek poet has the method of using the higher conceptions of the gods against the lower found more
complete expression than in Euripides.   And in so far,
too, he is still entirely on the ground of popular belief.
But at the same time it is characteristic of him that
he is familiar with and highly influenced by Greek
science.   He knows the most eminent representatives of Ionian naturalism (with the exception of
Democritus), and he is fond of displaying his knowledge.   Nevertheless, it cannot be said that he uses
it in a contentious spirit against popular belief ; on
the contrary, he is inclined in agreement with the
old philosophers to identify the gods of popular

belief with the elements. Towards sophistic he takes a similar, but less sympathetic attitude. Sophistic was not in vogue till he was a man of mature age ; he made acquaintance with it, and he made use of it—there are reflections in his dramas which carry distinct evidence of sophistic influence ; but in his treatment of religious problems he is not a disciple of the sophists, and on this subject, as on others, he occasionally attacked them.

It is against this background that we must set the reflections with an atheistic tone that we find in Euripides. They are, as already mentioned, rare ; indeed, strictly speaking there is only one case in which a character openly denies the existence of the gods. The passage is a fragment of the drama *Bellerophon* ; it is, despite its isolation, so typical of the manner of Euripides that it deserves to be quoted in full.

"And then to say that there are gods in the heavens ! Nay, there are none there ; if you are not foolish enough to be seduced by the old talk. Think for yourselves about the matter, and do not be influenced by my words. I contend that the tyrants kill the people wholesale, take their money and destroy cities in spite of their oaths ; and although they do all this they are happier than people who, in peace and quietness, lead god-fearing lives. And I know small states which honour the gods, but must obey greater states, which are less pious, because their spearmen are fewer in number. And I believe that you, if a slothful man just prayed to the gods and did not earn his bread by the work of his hands——" Here the sense is interrupted ;

5

but there remains one more line : " That which builds the castle of the gods is in part the unfortunate happenings . . ." The continuation is missing.

The argumentation here is characteristic of Euripides. From the injustice of life he infers the non-existence of the gods. The conclusion evidently only holds good on the assumption that the gods must be just ; and this is precisely one of the postulates of popular belief. The reasoning is not sophistic ; on the contrary, in their attacks the sophists took up a position outside the foundation of popular belief and attacked the foundation itself. This reasoning, on the other hand, is closely allied to the earlier religious thinking of the Greeks ; it only proceeds further than the latter, where it results in rank denial.

The drama of *Bellerophon* is lost, and reconstruction is out of the question ; if only for that reason it is unwarrantable to draw any conclusions from the detached fragment as to the poet's personal attitude towards the existence of the gods. But, nevertheless, the fragment is of interest in this connexion. It would never have occurred to Sophocles or Aeschylus to put such a speech in the mouth of one of his characters. When Euripides does that it is a proof that the question of the existence of the gods has begun to present itself to the popular consciousness at this time. Viewed in this light other statements of his which are not in themselves atheistic become significant. When it is said : " If the gods act in a shameful way, they are not gods "—that indeed is not atheism in our sense, but it is very near to it. Interesting is also the introduction to the drama *Melanippe* : " Zeus, whoever Zeus may be ; for of that I only know what is told." Aeschylus begins a strophe in one of his most famous choral odes with almost the same words : " Zeus, whoe'er he be ; for if he desire so to be called, I will address him by this name." In him it is an expression of genuine antique piety, which excludes all human impertinence towards the gods to such a degree that it even forgoes knowing their real names. In Euripides the same idea becomes an expression of doubt ; but in this case also the doubt is raised on the foundation of popular belief.

It is not surprising that so prominent and sustained a criticism of popular belief as that of Euripides, produced, moreover, on the stage, called forth a reaction from the defenders of the established faith, and that charges of impiety were not wanting. It is more to be wondered at that these charges on the whole are so few and slight, and that Euripides did not become the object of any actual prosecution. We know of a private trial in which the accuser incidentally charged Euripides with impiety on the strength of a quotation from one of his tragedies, Euripides's answer being a protest against dragging his poetry into the affair ; the verdict on that belonged to another court. Aristophanes, who is always severe on Euripides, has only one passage directly charging him with being a propagator of atheism ; but the accusation is hardly meant to be taken seriously. In *The Frogs*, where he had every opportunity of emphasising this view, there is hardly an indication of it. In *The Clouds*, where the main attack is directed against modern free-thought,

Euripides, to be sure, is sneered at as being the fashionable poet of the corrupted youth, but he is not drawn into the charge of impiety. Even when Plato wrote his *Republic*, Euripides was generally considered the " wisest of all tragedians." This would have been impossible if he had been considered an atheist. In spite of all, the general feeling must undoubtedly have been that Euripides ultimately took his stand on the ground of popular belief. It was a similar instinctive judgment in regard to religion which prevented antiquity from placing Xenophanes amongst the atheists. Later times no doubt judged differently ; the quotation from *Melanippe* is in fact cited as a proof that Euripides was an atheist in his heart of hearts.

In Aristophanes we meet with the first observations concerning the change in the religious conditions of Athens during the Peloponnesian War. In one of his plays, *The Clouds*, he actually set himself the task of taking up arms against modern unbelief, and he characterises it directly as atheism. If only for that reason the play deserves somewhat fuller consideration.

It is well known that Aristophanes chose Socrates as a representative of the modern movement. In him he embodies all the faults with which he wished to pick a quarrel in the fashionable philosophy of the day. On the other hand, the essence of Socratic teaching is entirely absent from Aristophanes's representation ; of that he had hardly any understanding, and even if he had he would at any rate not have been able to make use of it in his drama. We need not then in this connexion consider Socrates himself at all ; on the other hand, the play gives a good idea of the popular idea of sophistic. Here we find all the features of the school, grotesquely mixed up and distorted by the farce, it is true, but nevertheless easily recognisable : rhetoric as an end in itself, of course, with emphasis on its immoral aspect ; empty and hair-splitting dialectics ; linguistic researches ; Ionic naturalism ; and first and last, as the focus of all, denial of the gods. That Aristophanes was well informed on certain points, at any rate, is clear from the fact that the majority of the scientific explanations which he puts into the mouth of Socrates actually represent the latest results of science at that time—which in all probability did not prevent his Athenians from considering them as exceedingly absurd and ridiculous.

What matters here, however, is only the accusation of atheism which he made against Socrates. It is a little difficult to handle, in so far as Aristophanes, for dramatic reasons, has equipped Socrates with a whole set of deities. There are the clouds themselves, which are of Aristophanes's own invention ; there is also the air, which he has got from Diogenes of Apollonia, and finally a " vortex " which is supposed to be derived from the same source, and which at any rate has cast Zeus down from his throne. All this we must ignore, as it is only conditioned partly by technical reasons— Aristophanes had to have a chorus and chose the clouds for the purpose—and partially by the desire to ridicule Ionic naturalism. But enough is left over. In the beginning of the play Socrates expressly declares that no gods exist. Similar statements are repeated in several places. Zeus is sometimes substituted for the gods, but it comes to the same thing. And at the end of the play, where the honest Athenian, who has ventured on the ticklish ground of sophistic, admits his delusion, it is expressly said :

" Oh, what a fool I am ! Nay, I must have been mad indeed when I thought of throwing the gods away for Socrates's sake ! "

Even in the verses with which the chorus conclude the play it is insisted that the worst crime of the sophists is their insult to the gods.

The inference to be drawn from all this is simply that the popular Athenian opinion—for we may rest assured that this and the view of Aristophanes are identical—was that the sophists were atheists. That says but little. For popular opinion always works with broad categories, and the probability is that in this case, as demonstrated above, it was in the wrong, for, as a rule, the sophists were hardly conscious deniers of the gods. But, at the same time, at the back of the onslaught of Aristophanes there lies the idea that the teaching of the sophists led to denial of the gods ; that atheism was the natural outcome of their doctrine and way of reasoning. And that there was some truth therein is proved by other evidence which can hardly be rejected.

In the indictment of Socrates it is said that he " offended by not believing in the gods in which the State believed." In the two apologies for Socrates which have come down to us under Xenophon's

name, the author treats this accusation entirely
under the aspect of atheism, and tries to refute it
by positive proofs of the piety of Socrates. But
not one word is said about there being, in and for
itself, anything remarkable or improbable in the
charge. In Plato's *Apology*, Plato makes Socrates
ask the accuser point-blank whether he is of the
opinion that he, Socrates, does not believe in the
gods at all and accordingly is a downright denier
of the gods, or whether he merely means to say that
he believes in other gods than those of the State.
He makes the accuser answer that the assertion is
that Socrates does not believe in any gods at all.
In Plato Socrates refutes the accusation indirectly,
using a line of argument entirely differing from that
of Xenophon. But in Plato, too, the accusation
is treated as being in no way extraordinary. In
my opinion, Plato's *Apology* cannot be used as
historical evidence for details unless special reasons
can be given proving their historical value beyond
the fact that they occur in the *Apology*. But in
this connexion the question is not what was said or
not said at Socrates's trial. The decisive point is
that we possess two quite independent and unam-
biguous depositions by two fully competent witnesses of the beginning of the fourth century which
both treat of the charge of atheism as something
which is neither strange nor surprising at their time.
It is therefore permissible to conclude that in Athens
at this time there really existed circles or at any rate
not a few individuals who had given up the belief
in the popular gods.

A dialogue between Socrates and a young man

by name Aristodemus, given in Xenophon's *Memorabilia*, makes the same impression. Of Aristodemus it is said that he does not sacrifice to the gods, does not consult the Oracle and ridicules those who do so. When he is called to account for this behaviour he maintains that he does not despise " the divine," but is of the opinion that it is too exalted to need his worship. Moreover, he contends that the gods do not trouble themselves about mankind. This is, of course, not atheism in our sense ; but Aristodemus's attitude is, nevertheless, extremely eccentric in a community like that of Athens in the fifth century. And yet it is not mentioned as anything isolated and extraordinary, but as if it were something which, to be sure, was out of the common, but not unheard of.

It is further to be observed that at the end of the fifth century we often hear of active sacrilegious outrages. An example is the historic trial of Alcibiades for profanation of the Mysteries. But this was not an isolated occurrence ; there were more of the same kind at the time. Of the dithyrambic poet Cinesias it is said that he profaned holy things in an obscene manner. But the greatest stress of all must be laid on the well-known mutilation of the Hermae at Athens in 415, just before the expedition to Sicily. All the tales about the outrages of the Mysteries *may* have been fictitious, but it is a fact that the Hermae were mutilated. The motive was probably political : the members of a secret society intended to pledge themselves to each other by all committing a capital crime. But that they chose just this form of crime shows quite clearly that respect for the State religion had greatly declined in these circles.

What has so far been adduced as proof that the belief in the gods had begun to waver in Athens at the end of the fifth century is, in my opinion, conclusive in itself to anybody who is familiar with the more ancient Greek modes of thought and expression on this point, and can not only hear what is said, but also understand how it is said and what is passed over in silence.   Of course it can always be objected that the proofs are partly the assertions of a comic poet who certainly was not particular about accusations of impiety, partly deductions *ex silentio*, partly actions the motives for which are uncertain. Fortunately, however, we have—from a slightly later period, it is true—a positive utterance which confirms our conclusion and which comes from a man who was not in the habit of talking idly and who had the best opportunities of knowing the circumstances.

In the tenth book of his *Laws*, written shortly before his death, *i.e.* about the middle of the fourth century, Plato gives a detailed account of the question of irreligion seen from the point of view of penal legislation.   He distinguishes here between three forms, namely, denial of the existence of the gods, denial of the divine providence (whereas the existence of the gods is admitted), and finally the assumption that the gods exist and exercise providence, but that they allow themselves to be influenced by sacrifices and prayers.   Of these three categories the last is evidently directed against ancient popular belief itself ; it does not therefore interest us in this connexion. The second view, the denial of a providence, we have already met with in Xenophon in the character of Aristodemus, and in the sophist Thrasymachus; Euripides, too, sometimes alludes to it, though it was far from being his own opinion. Whether it amounted to denial of the gods or not was, in ancient times, the cause of much dispute; it is, of course, not atheism in our sense, but it is certainly evidence that belief in the gods is shaken. The first view, on the other hand, is sheer atheism. Plato consequently reckons with this as a serious danger to the community; he mentions it as a widespread view among the youth of his time, and in his legislation he sentences to death those who fail to be converted. It would seem certain, therefore, that there was, in reality, something in it after all.

Plato does not confine himself to defining atheism and laying down the penalty for it; he at the same time, in accordance with a principle which he generally follows in the *Laws*, discusses it and tries to disprove it. In this way he happens to give us information—which is of special interest to us—of the proofs which were adduced by its followers.

The argument is a twofold one. First comes the naturalistic proof; the heavenly bodies, according to the general (and Plato's own) view the most certain deities, are inanimate natural objects. It is interesting to note that in speaking of this doctrine in detail reference is clearly made to Anaxagoras; this confirms our afore-mentioned conjectures as to the character of his work. Plato was quite in a position to deal with Anaxagoras on the strength not only of what he said, but of what he passed over in silence. The second argument is the well-known sophistic one, that the gods are *nomôi*, not *physei*, they depend upon convention, which has nothing to do with reality. In this connexion the argument adds that what applies to the gods, applies also to right and wrong ; *i.e.* we find here in the *Laws* the view with which we are familiar from Callicles in the *Gorgias*, but with the missing link supplied. And Plato's development of this theme shows clearly just what a general historical consideration might lead us to expect, namely, that it was naturalism and sophistic that jointly undermined the belief in the old gods.

CHAPTER V

WITH Socrates and his successors the whole question of the relation of Greek thought to popular belief enters upon a new phase. The Socratic philosophy is in many ways a continuation of sophistic. This is involved already in the fact that the same questions form the central interest in the two schools of thought, so that the problems stated by the sophists became the decisive factor in the content of Socratic and Platonic thought. The Socratic schools at the same time took over the actual programme of the sophists, namely, the education of adolescence in the highest culture. But, on the other hand, the Socratic philosophy was in the opposite camp to sophistic; on many points it represents a reaction against it, a recollection of the valuable elements contained in earlier Greek thought on life, especially human life, values which sophistic regarded with indifference or even hostility, and which were threatened with destruction if it should carry the day. This reactionary tendency in Socratic philosophy appears nowhere more plainly than in the field of religion.

Under these circumstances it is a peculiar irony of fate that the very originator of the new trend in Greek thought was charged with and sentenced for impiety. We have already mentioned the singular prelude to the indictment afforded by the comedy of Aristophanes. We have also remarked upon the futility of looking therein for any actual enlightenment on the Socratic point of view. And Plato makes Socrates state this with all necessary sharpness in the *Apology*. Hence what we may infer from the attack of Aristophanes is merely this, that the general public lumped Socrates together with the sophists and more especially regarded him as a godless fellow. Unless this had been so, Aristophanes could not have introduced him as the chief character in his travesty. And without doubt it was this popular point of view which his accusers relied on when they actually included atheism as a count in their bill of indictment. It will, nevertheless, be necessary to dwell for a moment on this bill of indictment and the defence.

The charge of impiety was a twofold one, partly for not believing in the gods the State believed in, partly for introducing new "demonic things." This latter act was directly punishable according to Attic law. What his accusers alluded to was the *daimonion* of Socrates. That they should have had any idea of what that was must be regarded as utterly out of the question, and whatever it may have been —and of this we shall have a word to say later— it had at any rate nothing whatever to do with atheism. As to the charge of not believing in the gods of the State, Plato makes the accuser prefer it in the form that Socrates did not believe in any gods at all, after which it becomes an easy matter for Socrates to show that it is directly incompatible with the charge of introducing new deities. As ground for his accusation the accuser states—in Plato, as before—that Socrates taught the same doctrine about the sun and moon as Anaxagoras. The whole of the passage in the *Apology* in which the question of the denial of gods is dealt with—a short dialogue between Socrates and the accuser, quite in the Socratic manner — historically speaking, carries little conviction, and we therefore dare not take it for granted that the charge either of atheism or of false doctrine about the sun and moon was put forward in that form. But that something about this latter point was mentioned during the trial must be regarded as probable, when we consider that Xenophon, too, defends Socrates at some length against the charge of concerning himself with speculations on Nature. That he did not do so must be taken for certain, not only from the express evidence of Xenophon and Plato, but from the whole nature of the case. The accusation on this point was assuredly pure fabrication. There remains only what was no doubt also the main point, namely, the assertion of the pernicious influence of Socrates on the young, and the inference of ir-religion to be drawn from it—an argument which it would be absurd to waste any words upon.

The attack, then, affords no information about Socrates's personal point of view as regards belief in the gods, and the defence only very little. Both Xenophon and Plato give an account of Socrates's *daimonion*, but this point has so little relation to the charge of atheism that it is not worth examina-tion. For the rest Plato's defence is indirect. He makes Socrates refute his opponent, but does not let him say a word about his own point of view. Xenophon is more positive, in so far as in the first place he asserts that Socrates worshipped the gods like any other good citizen, and more especially that he advised his friends to use the Oracle ; in the second place, that, though he lived in full publicity, no one ever saw him do or heard him say anything of an impious nature. All these assertions are assuredly correct, and they render it highly improbable that Socrates should have secretly abandoned the popular faith, but ·they tell us little that is positive about his views. Fortunately we possess other means of getting to closer grips with the question ; the way must be through a consideration of Socrates's whole conduct and his mode of thought.

Here we at once come to the interesting negative fact that there is nothing in tradition to indicate that Socrates ever occupied himself with theological questions. To be sure, Xenophon has twice put into his mouth a whole theodicy expressing an elaborate teleological view of nature. But that we dare not base anything upon this is now, I think, universally acknowledged. Plato, in the dialogue *Euthyphron*, makes him subject the popular notion of piety to a devastating criticism ; but this, again, will not nowadays be regarded as historical by anybody. Everything we are told about Socrates which bears the stamp of historical truth indicates that he restricted himself to ethics and left theology alone. But this very fact is not without significance. It indicates that Socrates's aim was not to alter the religious views of his contemporaries. Since he did not do so we may reasonably believe it was because they did not inconvenience him in what was most important to him, *i.e.* ethics.

We may, however, perhaps go even a step farther. We may venture, I think, to maintain that so far from contemporary religion being a hindrance to Socrates in his occupation as a teacher of ethics, it was, on the contrary, an indispensable support to him, nay, an integral component of his fundamental ethical view. The object of Socrates in his relations with his fellow-men was, on his own showing—for on this important point I think we can confidently rely upon Plato's *Apology*—to make clear to them that they knew nothing. And when he was asked to say in what he himself differed from other people, he could mention only one thing, namely, that he was aware of his own ignorance. But his ignorance is not an ignorance of this thing or that, it is a radical ignorance, something involved in the essence of man as man. That is, in other words, it is determined by religion. In order to be at all intelligible and ethically applicable, it pre-supposes the conception of beings of whom the essence is knowledge. For Socrates and his con-temporaries the popular belief supplied such beings in the gods. The institution of the Oracle itself is an expression of the recognition of the superiority of the gods to man in knowledge. But the dogma had long been stated even in its absolute form when Homer said : " The gods know everything." To Socrates, who always took his starting-point quite popularly from notions that were universally ac-cepted, this basis was simply indispensable. And so far from inconveniencing Socrates, the multiplicity and anthropomorphism of the gods seemed an advantage to him—the more they were like man in all but the essential qualification, the better.

The Socratic ignorance has an ethical bearing. Its complement is his assertion that virtue is knowledge. Here again the gods are the necessary presupposition and determination. That the gods were good, or, as it was preferred to express it, " just " (the Greek word comprises more than the English word), was no less a popular dogma than the notion that they possessed knowledge. Now all Socrates's efforts were directed towards goodness as an end in view, towards the ethical development of mankind. Here again popular belief was his best ally. To the people to whom he talked, virtue (the Greek word is at once both wider and narrower in sense than the English term) was no mere abstract notion ; it was a living reality to them, embodied in beings that were like themselves, human beings, but perfect human beings.

If we correlate this with the negative circumstance that Socrates was no theologian but a teacher of ethics, we can easily understand a point of view which accepted popular belief as it was and employed it for working purposes in the service of moral teaching. Such a point of view, moreover, gained extraordinary strength by the fact that it preserved continuity with earlier Greek religious thought. This latter, too, had been ethical in its bearing ; it, too, had employed the gods in the service of its ethical aim. But its central idea was felicity, not virtue ; its starting-point was the popular dogma of the felicity

6

of the gods, not their justice. In this way it had come to lay stress on a virtue which might be termed modesty, but in a religious sense, *i.e.* man must recognise his difference from the gods as a limited being, subject to the vicissitudes of an existence above which the gods are raised. Socrates says just the same, only that he puts knowledge or virtue, which to him was the same thing, in the place of felicity. From a religious point of view the result is exactly the same, namely, the doctrine of the gods as the terminus and ideal, and the insistence on the gulf separating man from them. We are tempted to say that, had Socrates turned with hostile intent against a religion which thus played into his hands, the more fool he. But this is putting the problem the wrong way up—Socrates never stood critically outside popular belief and traditional religious thought speculating as to whether he should use it or reject it. No, his thought grew out of it as from the bosom of the earth. Hence its mighty religious power, its inevitable victory over a school of thought which had severed all connexion with tradition.

That such a point of view should be so badly misunderstood as it was in Athens seems incomprehensible. The explanation is no doubt that the whole story of Socrates's denial of the gods was only included by his accusers for the sake of completeness, and did not play any great part in the final issue. This seems confirmed by the fact that they found it convenient to support their charge of atheism by one of introducing foreign gods, this being punishable by Attic law. They thus obtained some slight hold for their accusation. But both charges must be presumed to have been so signally refuted during the trial that it is hardly possible that any great number of the judges were influenced by them. It was quite different and far weightier matters which brought about the conviction of Socrates, questions on which there was really a deep and vital difference of opinion between him and his contemporaries. That Socrates's attitude towards popular belief was at any rate fully understood elsewhere is testified by the answer of the Delphic Oracle, that declared Socrates to be the wisest of all men. However remarkable such a pronouncement from such a place may appear, it seems impossible to reject the accounts of it as unhistorical; on the other hand, it does not seem impossible to explain how the Oracle came to declare itself as reported. Earlier Greek thought, which insisted upon the gulf separating gods and men, was from olden times intimately connected with the Delphic Oracle. It hardly sprang from there; more probably it arose spontaneously in various parts of Hellas. But it would naturally feel attracted toward the Oracle, which was one of the religious centres of Hellas, and it was recognised as legitimate by the Oracle. Above all, the honour shown by the Oracle to Pindar, one of the chief representatives of the earlier thought, testifies to this. Hence there is nothing incredible in the assumption that Socrates attracted notice at Delphi as a defender of the old-fashioned religious views approved by the Oracle, precisely in virtue of his opposition to the ideas then in vogue.

If we accept this explanation we are, however,

excluded from taking literally Plato's account of
the answer of the Delphic Oracle and Socrates's
attitude towards it.   Plato presents the case as if
the Oracle were the starting-point of Socrates's
philosophy and of the peculiɪr mode of life which
was indissolubly bound up with it.   This presentation cannot be correct if we are to regard the Oracle
as historical and understand it as we have understood it.   The Oracle presupposes the Socrates we
know : a man with a religious message and a mode
of life which was bound to attract notice to him as an
exception from the general rule.   It cannot, therefore, have been the cause of Socrates's finding himself.
On the other hand, it is difficult to imagine a man
choosing a mode of life like that of Socrates without
a definite inducement, without some fact or other
that would lead him to conceive himself as an
exception from the rule.   If we look for such a fact
in the life of Socrates, we shall look in vain as regards
externals.   Apart from his activities as a religious
and ethical personality, his life was that of any other
Attic citizen.   But in his spiritual life there was
certainly one point, but only one, on which he
deviated from the normal, namely, his *daimonion*.
If we examine the accounts of this more closely the
only thing we can make of them is—or so at least it
seems to me—that we are here in the presence of a
form—peculiar, no doubt, and highly developed—of
the phenomena which are nowadays classed under
the concept of clairvoyance.   Now Plato makes
Socrates himself say that the power of avoiding what
would harm him, in great things and little, by virtue
of a direct perception (a " voice "), which is what

constituted his *daimonion*, was given him from childhood. That it was regarded as something singular both by himself and others is evident, and likewise that he himself regarded it as something supernatural; the designation *daimonion* itself seems to be his own. I think that we must seek for the origin of Socrates's peculiar mode of life in this direction, strange as it may be that a purely mystic element should have given the impulse to the most rationalistic philosophy the world has ever produced. It is impossible to enter more deeply into this problem here ; but, if my conjecture is correct, we have an additional explanation of the fact that Socrates was disposed to anything rather than an attack on the established religion.

A view of popular religion such as I have here sketched bore in itself the germ of a further development which must lead in other directions. A personality like Socrates might perhaps manage throughout a lifetime to keep that balance on a razor's edge which is involved in utilising to the utmost in the service of ethics the popular dogmas of the perfection of the gods, while disregarding all irrelevant tales, all myths and all notions of too human a tenor about them. This demanded concentration on the one thing needful, in conjunction with deep piety of the most genuine antique kind, with the most profound religious modesty, a combination which it was assuredly given to but one man to attain. Socrates's successors had it not. Starting precisely from a Socratic foundation they entered upon theological speculations which carried them away from the Socratic point of view.

For the Cynics, who set up virtue as the only good, the popular notions of the gods would seem to have been just as convenient as for Socrates. And we know that Antisthenes, the founder of the school, made ample use of them in his ethical teaching. He represented Heracles as the Cynical ideal and occupied himself largely with allegorical interpretation of the myths. On the other hand, there is a tradition that he maintained that " according to nature " there was only one god, but " according to the law " several—a purely sophistic view. He inveighed against the worship of images, too, and maintained that god " did not resemble any thing," and we know that his school rejected all worship of the gods because the gods " were in need of nothing." This conception, too, is presumably traceable to Antisthenes. In all this the theological interest is evident. As soon as this interest sets in, the harmonious relation to the popular faith is upset, the discord between its higher and lower ideas becomes manifest, and criticism begins to assert itself. In the case of Antisthenes, if we may believe tradition, it seems to have led to monotheism, in itself a most remarkable phenomenon in the history of Greek religion, but the material is too slight for us to make anything of it. The later Cynics afford interesting features in illustration of atheism in antiquity, but this is best left to a later chapter.

About the relations of the Megarians to the popular faith we know next to nothing. One of them, Stilpo, was charged with impiety on account of a bad joke about Athene, and convicted, although he tried to save himself by another bad joke. As his point of view was that of a downright sceptic, he was no doubt an atheist according to the notions of antiquity ; in our day he would be called an agnostic, but the information that we have about his religious standpoint is too slight to repay dwelling on him.

As to the relation of the Cyrenaic school to the popular faith, the general proposition has been handed down to us that the wise man could not be " deisidaimon," *i.e.* superstitious or god-fearing ; the Greek word can have both senses. This does not speak for piety at any rate, but then the relationship of the Cyrenaics to the gods of popular belief was different from that of the other followers of Socrates. As they set up pleasure—the momentary, isolated feeling of pleasure—as the supreme good, they had no use for the popular conceptions of the gods in their ethics, nay, these conceptions were even a hindrance to them in so far as the fear of the gods might prove a restriction where it ought not to. In these circumstances we cannot wonder at finding a member of the school in the list of *atheoi*. This is Theodorus of Cyrene, who lived about the year 300. He really seems to have been a downright denier of the gods ; he wrote a work *On the Gods* containing a searching criticism of theology, which is said to have exposed him to unpleasantness during a stay at Athens, but the then ruler of the city, Demetrius of Phalerum, protected him. There is nothing strange in a manifestation of downright atheism at this time and from this quarter. More remarkable is that interest in theology which we must assume Theodorus to have had, since he wrote at length upon the subject. Unfortunately it is not evident from the account whether his criticism was directed mostly against popular religion or against the theology of the philosophers. As it was asserted in antiquity that Epicurus used his book largely, the latter is more probable.

Whereas in the case of the " imperfect Socratics " as well as of all the earlier philosophers we must content ourselves with more or less casual notes, and at the best with fragments, and for Socrates with second-hand information, when we come to Plato we find ourselves for the first time in the presence of full and authentic information. Plato belongs to those few among the ancient authors of whom everything that their contemporaries possessed has been preserved to our own day. There would, however, be no cause to speak about Plato in an investigation of atheism in antiquity, had not so eminent a scholar as Zeller roundly asserted that Plato did not believe in the Greek gods—with the exception of the heavenly bodies, in the case of which the facts are obvious. On the other hand, it is impossible here to enter upon a close discussion of so large a question ; I must content myself with giving my views in their main lines, with a brief statement of my reasons for holding them.

In the mythical portions of his dialogues Plato uses the gods as a given poetic motive and treats them with poetic licence. Otherwise they play a very inferior part in the greater portion of his works. In the *Euthyphron* he gives a sharp criticism of the popular conception of piety, and in reality at the same time very seriously questions the importance and value of the existing form of worship. In his chief ethical work, the *Gorgias*, he subjects the fundamental problems of individual ethics to a close discussion without saying one word of their relation to religion ; if we except the mythic part at the end the gods scarcely appear in the dialogue. Finally, in his *Republic* he no doubt gives a detailed criticism of popular mythology as an element of education, and in the course of this also some positive definitions of the idea of God, but throughout the construction of his ideal community he entirely disregards religion and worship, even if he occasionally takes it for granted that a cult of some sort exists, and in one place quite casually refers to the Oracle at Delphi as authority for its organisation in details. To this may further be added the negative point that he never in any of his works made Socrates define his position in regard to the sophistic treatment of the popular religion.

In Plato's later works the case is different. In the construction of the universe described in the *Timaeus* the gods have a definite and significant place, and in the *Laws*, Plato's last work, they play a leading part. Here he not only gives elaborate rules for the organisation of the worship which permeate the whole life of the community, but even in the argument of the dialogue the gods are everywhere in evidence in a way which strongly suggests bigotry. Finally, Plato gives the above-mentioned definitions of impiety and fixes the severest punishment for it—for downright denial of the gods, when all attempts at conversion have failed, the penalty of death.

On this evidence we are tempted to take the view that Plato in his earlier years took up a critical attitude in regard to the gods of popular belief, perhaps even denied them altogether, that he gradually grew more conservative, and ended by being a confirmed bigot.   And we might look for a corroboration of this in a peculiar observation in the *Laws*.   Plato opens his admonition to the young against atheism by reminding them that they are young, and that false opinion concerning the gods is a common disease among the young, but that utter denial of their existence is not wont to endure to old age.   In this we might see an expression of personal religious experience.

Nevertheless I do not think such a construction of Plato's religious development feasible.   A decisive objection is his exposition of the Socratic point of view in so early a work as the *Apology*.   I at any rate regard it as psychologically impossible that a downright atheist, be he ever so great a poet, should be able to draw such a picture of a deeply religious personality, and draw it with so much sympathy and such convincing force.   Add to this other facts of secondary moment.   Even the close criticism to which Plato subjects the popular notions of the gods in his *Republic* does not indicate denial of the gods as such ; moreover, it is built on a positive foundation, on the idea of the goodness of the gods and their truth (which for Plato manifests itself in immutability).   Finally, Plato at all times vigorously advocated the belief in providence.   In the *Laws* he stamps unbelief in divine providence as impiety ; in the *Republic* he insists in a prominent passage that the gods love the just man and order everything for him in the best way. And he puts the same thought into Socrates's mouth in the *Apology*, though it is hardly Socratic in the strict sense of the word, *i.e.* as a main point in Socrates's conception of existence. All this should warn us not to exaggerate the significance of the difference which may be pointed out between the religious standpoints of the younger and the older Plato. But the difference itself cannot, I think, be denied ; there can hardly be any doubt that Plato was much more critical of popular belief in his youth and prime than towards the close of his life.

Even in Plato's later works there is, in spite of their conservative attitude, a very peculiar reservation in regard to the anthropomorphic gods of popular belief. It shows itself in the *Laws* in the fact that where he sets out to *prove* the existence of the gods he contents himself with proving the divinity of the heavenly bodies and quite disregards the other gods. It appears still more plainly in the *Timaeus*, where he gives a philosophical explanation of how the divine heavenly bodies came into existence, but says expressly of the other gods that such an explanation is impossible, and that we must abide by what the old theologians said on this subject ; they being partly the children of gods would know best where their parents came from. It is observations of this kind that induced Zeller to believe that Plato altogether denied the gods of popular belief ; he also contends that the gods have no place in Plato's system. This latter contention is perfectly correct ; Plato never identified the gods with the ideas (although he comes very near to it in the *Republic*, where he attributes to them immutability, the quality which determines the essence of the ideas), and in the *Timaeus* he distinguishes sharply between them. No doubt his doctrine of ideas led up to a kind of divinity, the idea of the good, as the crown of the system, but the direct inference from this conception would be pure monotheism and so exclude polytheism. This inference Plato did not draw, though his treatment of the gods in the *Laws* and *Timaeus* certainly shows that he was quite clear that the gods of the popular faith were an irrational element in his conception of the universe. The two passages do not entitle us to go further and conclude that he utterly rejected them, and in the *Timaeus*, where Plato makes both classes of gods, both the heavenly bodies and the others, take part in the creation of man, this is plainly precluded. The playful turn with which he evades inquiry into the origin of the gods thus receives its proper limitation; it is entirely confined to their origin.

Such, according to my view, is the state of the case. It is of fundamental importance to emphasise the fact that we cannot conclude, because the gods of popular belief do not fit into the system of a philosopher, that he denies their existence. In what follows we shall have occasion to point out a case in which, as all are now agreed, a philosophical school has adopted and stubbornly held to the belief in the existence of gods though this assumption was directly opposed to a fundamental proposition in its system of doctrine. The case of Plato is particularly interesting because he himself was aware and has pointed out that here was a point on which the consistent scientific application of his conception of the universe must fail. It is the outcome—one of many—of what is perhaps his finest quality as a philosopher, namely, his intellectual honesty.

An indirect testimony to the correctness of the view here stated will be found in the way in which Plato's faithful disciple Xenocrates developed his theology, for it shows that Xenocrates presupposed the existence of the gods of popular belief as given by Plato. Xenocrates made it his general task to systematise Plato's philosophy (which had never been set forth publicly by himself as a whole), and to secure it against attack. In the course of this work he was bound to discover that the conception of the gods of popular belief was a particularly weak point in Plato's system, and he attempted to mend matters by a peculiar theory which became of the greatest importance for later times. Xenocrates set up as gods, in the first place, the heavenly bodies. Next he gave his highest principles (pure abstracts such as oneness and twoness) and the elements of his universe (air, water and earth) the names of some of the highest divinities in popular belief (Zeus, Hades, Poseidon, Demeter). These gods, however, did not enter into direct communication with men, but only through some intermediate agent. The intermediate agents were the " demons," a class of beings who were higher than man yet not perfect like the gods. They were, it seems, immortal ; they were invisible and far more powerful than human beings ; but they were subject to human passions and were of highly differing

grades of moral perfection. These are the beings
that are the objects of the greater part of the existing
cult, especially such usages as rest on the assumption
that the gods can do harm and are directed towards
averting it, or which are in other ways objectionable ; and with them are connected the myths which
Plato subjected to so severe a criticism. Xenocrates found a basis for this system in Plato, who
in the *Symposium* sets up the demons as a class of
beings between gods and men, and makes them
carriers of the prayers and wishes of men to the
gods. But what was a passing thought with Plato
serving only a poetical purpose was taken seriously
and systematised by Xenocrates.

It can hardly be said that Xenocrates has
gained much recognition among modern writers on
the history of philosophy for his theory of demons.
And yet I cannot see that there was any other
possible solution of the problem which ancient
popular belief set ancient philosophy, if, be it understood, we hold fast by two hypotheses : the first,
that the popular belief and worship of the ancients
was based throughout on a foundation of reality ;
and second, that moral perfection is an essential
factor in the conception of God. The only inconsistency which we may perhaps bring home to
Xenocrates is that he retained certain of the
popular names of the gods as designations for gods
in his sense ; but this inconsistency was, as we shall
see, subsequently removed. In favour of this
estimate of Xenocrates's doctrine of demons may
further be adduced that it actually was the last
word of ancient philosophy on the matter. The

doctrine was adopted by the Stoics, the Neo-Pythagoreans, and the Neo-Platonists. Only the Epicureans went another way, but their doctrine died out before the close of antiquity. And so the doctrine of demons became the ground on which Jewish-Christian monotheism managed to come to terms with ancient paganism, to conquer it in theory, as it were.

This implies, however, that the doctrine of demons, though it arose out of an honest attempt to save popular belief philosophically, in reality brings out its incompatibility with philosophy. The religion and worship of the ancients could dispense with neither the higher nor the lower conceptions of its gods. If the former were done away with, recognition, however full, of the existence of the gods was no good ; in the long run the inference could not be avoided that they were immoral powers and so ought not to be worshipped. This was the inference drawn by Christianity in theory and enforced in practice, ultimately by main force.

Aristotle is among the philosophers who were prosecuted for impiety. When the anti-Macedonian party came into power in Athens after the death of Alexander, there broke out a persecution against his adherents, and this was also directed against Aristotle. The basis of the charge against him was that he had shown divine honour after his death to the tyrant Hermias, whose guest he had been during a prolonged stay in Asia Minor. This seems to have been a fabrication, and at any rate has nothing to do with atheism. In the writings of Aristotle, as they were then generally known, it would assuredly have been impossible to find any ground for a charge of atheism.

Nevertheless, Aristotle is one of the philosophers about whose faith in the gods of popular religion well-founded doubts may be raised. Like Plato, he acknowledged the divinity of the heavenly bodies on the ground that they must have a soul since they had independent motion. Further, he has a kind of supreme god who, himself unmoved, is the cause of all movement, and whose constituent quality is reason. As regards the gods of popular belief, in his *Ethics* and his *Politics* he assumes public worship to be a necessary constituent of the life of the individual and the community. He gave no grounds for this assumption—on the contrary, he expressly declared that it was a question which ought not to be discussed at all : he who stirs up doubts whether honour should be paid to the gods is in need not of teaching but of punishment. (That he himself took part in worship is evident from his will.) Further, in his ethical works he used the conceptions of the gods almost in the same way as we have assumed that Socrates did, *i.e.* as the ethical ideal and determining the limits of the human. He never entered upon any elaborate criticism of the lower elements of popular religion such as Plato gave. So far everything is in admirable order. But if we look more closely at things there is nevertheless nearly always a little " but " in Aristotle's utterances about the gods. Where he operates with popular notions he prefers to speak hypothetically or to refer to what is generally assumed ; or he is content to use only definitions which will also agree with his

own philosophical conception of God.   But he goes
further ; in a few places in his writings there are
utterances which it seems can only be interpreted
as a radical denial of the popular religion.   The most
important of them deserves to be quoted *in extenso* :

" A tradition has been handed down from
the ancients and from the most primitive times,
and left to later ages in the form of myth, that
these substances (*i.e.* sky and heavenly bodies)
are gods and that the divine embraces all
nature.   The rest consists in legendary additions
intended to impress the multitude and serve the
purposes of legislation and the common weal ; for
these gods are said to have human shape or resemble
certain other beings (animals), and they say other
things which follow from this and are of a similar
kind to those already mentioned.   But if we disregard all this and restrict ourselves to the first
point, that they thought that the first substances
were gods, we must acknowledge that it is a divinely
inspired saying.   And as, in all probability, every
art and science has been discovered many times, as
far as it is possible, and has perished again, so these
notions, too, may have been preserved till now as
relics of those times.   To this extent only can we
have any idea of the opinion which was held by our
fathers and has come down from the beginning of
things."

The last sentences, expressing Aristotle's idea of
a life-cycle and periods of civilisation which repeat
themselves, have only been included in the quotation
for the sake of completeness.   If we disregard them,
the passage plainly enough states the view that the

7

only element of truth in the traditional notions about the gods was the divinity of the sky and the heavenly bodies ; the rest is myth. Aristotle has nowhere else expressed himself with such distinctness and in such length, but then the passage in question has a place of its own. It comes in his *Metaphysics* directly after the exposition of his philosophical conception of God—a position marked by profound earnestness and as it were irradiated by a quiet inner fervour. We feel that we are here approaching the *sanctum sanctorum* of the thinker. In this connexion, and only here, he wished for once to state his opinion about the religion of his time without reserve. What he says here is a precise formulation of the result arrived at by the best Greek thinkers as regards the religion of the Greek people. It was not, they thought, pure fabrication. It contained an element of truth of the greatest value. But most of it consisted of human inventions without any reality behind them.

A point of view like that of Aristotle would, I suppose, hardly have been called atheism among the ancients, if only because the heavenly bodies were acknowledged as divine. But according to our definition it is atheism. The " sky "-gods of Aristotle have nothing in common with the gods of popular belief, not even their names, for Aristotle never names them. And the rest, the whole crowd of Greek anthropomorphic gods, exist only in the human imagination.

Aristotle's successors offer little of interest to our inquiry. Theophrastus was charged with impiety, but the charge broke down completely.

His theological standpoint was certainly the same as Aristotle's. Of Strato, the most independent of the Peripatetics, we know that in his view of nature he laid greater stress on the material causes than Aristotle did, and so arrived at a different conception of the supreme deity. Aristotle had severed the deity from Nature and placed it outside the latter as an incorporeal being whose chief determining factor was reason. In Strato's view the deity was identical with Nature and, like the latter, was without consciousness ; consciousness was only found in organic nature. Consequently we cannot suppose him to have believed in the divinity of the heavenly bodies in Aristotle's sense, though no direct statement on this subject has come down to us. About his attitude towards popular belief we hear nothing. A denial of the popular gods is not necessarily implied in Strato's theory, but seems reasonable in itself and is further rendered probable by the fact that all writers seem to take it for granted that Strato knew no god other than the whole of Nature.

We designated Socratic philosophy, in its relation to popular belief, as a reaction against the radical free-thought of the sophistic movement. It may seem peculiar that with Aristotle it develops into a view which we can only describe as atheism. There is, however, an important difference between the standpoints of the sophists and of Aristotle. Radical as the latter is at bottom, it is not, however, openly opposed to popular belief—on the contrary, to any one who did not examine it more closely it must have had the appearance of accepting popular belief. The very assumption that the heavenly bodies were divine would contribute to that effect ; this, as we have seen, was a point on which the popular view laid great stress. If we add to this that Aristotle never made the existence of the popular gods matter of debate ; that he expressly acknowledged the established worship ; and that he consistently made use of certain fundamental notions of popular belief in his philosophy—we can hardly avoid the conclusion that, notwithstanding his personal emancipation from the existing religion, he is a true representative of the Socratic reaction against sophistic. But we see, too, that there is a reservation in this reaction. In continuity with earlier Greek thought on religion, it proceeded from the absolute definitions of the divine offered by popular belief, but when criticising anthropomorphism on this basis it did not after all avoid falling out with popular belief. How far each philosopher went in his antagonism was a matter of discretion, as also was the means chosen to reconcile the philosophical with the popular view. The theology of the Socratic schools thus suffered from a certain half-heartedness ; in the main it has the character of a compromise. It would not give up the popular notions of the gods, and yet they were continually getting in the way. This dualism governs the whole of the succeeding Greek philosophy.

CHAPTER VI

DURING the three or four centuries which passed between the downfall of free Hellas and the beginning of the Roman Empire, great social and political changes took place in the ancient world, involving also vital changes in religion. The chief phenomenon in this field, the invasion of foreign, especially oriental, religions into Hellas, does not come within the scope of this investigation. On the one hand, it is an expression of dissatisfaction with the old gods ; on the other, the intrusion of new gods would contribute to the ousting of the old ones. There is no question of atheism here ; it is only a change within polytheism. But apart from this change there is evidence that the old faith had lost its hold on men's minds to no inconsiderable extent. Here, too, there is hardly any question of atheism properly speaking, but as a background to the—not very numerous — evidences of such atheism in our period, we cannot well ignore the decline of the popular faith. Our investigation is rendered difficult on this point, and generally within this period, by the lack of direct evidence. Of the rich Hellenistic literature almost everything has been lost, and we are restricted to reports and fragments.

In order to gain a concrete starting-point we

will begin with a quotation from the historian
Polybius—so to speak the only Greek prose author
of the earlier Hellenistic period of whose works
considerable and connected portions are preserved.
Polybius wrote in the latter half of the second century a history of the world in which Rome took the
dominant place. Here he gave, among other things,
a detailed description of the Roman constitution
and thus came to touch upon the state of religion in
Rome as compared with that in Greece. He says
on this subject :

" The greatest advantage of the Roman constitution seems to me to lie in its conception of the
gods, and I believe that what among other peoples is
despised is what holds together the Roman power
—I mean superstition. For this feature has by
them been developed so far in the direction of
the ' horrible,' and has so permeated both private
and public life, that it is quite unique. Many
will perhaps find this strange, but I think they
have acted so with an eye to the mass of the people.
For if it were possible to compose a state of reasonable people such a procedure would no doubt be
unnecessary, but as every people regarded as a mass
is easily impressed and full of criminal instincts,
unreasonable violence, and fierce passion, there is
nothing to be done but to keep the masses under by
vague fears and such-like hocus-pocus. Therefore
it is my opinion that it was not without good
reason or by mere chance that the ancients imparted to the masses the notions of the gods and the
underworld, but rather is it thoughtless and irrational when nowadays we seek to destroy them."

As a proof of this last statement follows a comparison between the state of public morals in Greece and in Rome. In Greece you cannot trust a man with a few hundred pounds without ten notaries and as many seals and double the number of witnesses; in Rome great public treasure is administered with honesty merely under the safeguard of an oath.

As we see, this passage contains direct evidence that in the second century in Hellas—in contradistinction to Rome—there was an attempt to break down the belief in the gods. By his " we " Polybius evidently referred especially to the leading political circles. He knew these circles from personal experience, and his testimony has all the more weight because he does not come forward in the rôle of the orthodox man complaining in the usual way of the impiety of his contemporaries; on the contrary, he speaks as the educated and enlightened man to whom it is a matter of course that all this talk about the gods and the underworld is a myth which nobody among the better classes takes seriously. This is a tone we have not heard before, and it is a strong indirect testimony to the fact that Polybius is not wrong when he speaks of disbelief among the upper classes of Greece.

In this connexion the work of Polybius has a certain interest on another point. Where earlier —and later—authors would speak of the intervention of the gods in the march of history, he operates as a rule with an idea which he calls Tyche. The word is untranslatable when used in this way. It is something between chance, fortune and fate. It is more comprehensive and more personal than chance; it has not the immutable, the "lawbound" character of fate; rather it denotes the incalculability, the capriciousness associated, especially in earlier usage, with the word fortune, but without the tendency of this word to be used in a good sense.

This Tyche-religion—if we may use this expression—was not new in Hellas. Quite early we find Tyche worshipped as a goddess among the other deities, and it is an old notion that the gods send good fortune, a notion which set its mark on a series of established phrases in private and public life. But what is of interest here is that shifting of religious ideas in the course of which Tyche drives the gods into the background. We find indications of it as early as Thucydides. In his view of history he lays the main stress, certainly, on human initiative, and not least on rational calculation, as the cause of events. But where he is obliged to reckon with an element independent of human efforts, he calls it Tyche and not "the immortal gods." A somewhat similar view we find in another great political author of the stage of transition to our period, namely, Demosthenes. Demosthenes of course employs the official apparatus of gods: he invokes them on solemn occasions; he quotes their authority in support of his assertions (once he even reported a revelation which he had in a dream); he calls his opponents enemies of the gods, etc. But in his political considerations the gods play a negligible part. The factors with which he reckons as a rule are merely political forces. Where he is compelled to bring forward elements which man cannot control, he shows a preference for Tyche. He certainly occasionally identifies her with the favour of the gods, but in such a way as to give the impression that it is only a *façon de parler*. Direct pronouncements of a free-thinking kind one would not expect from an orator and statesman, and yet Demosthenes was once bold enough to say that Pythia, the mouthpiece of the Delphic Oracle, was a partisan of Macedonia, an utterance which his opponent Aeschines, who liked to parade ` his orthodoxy, did not omit to cast in his teeth. On the whole, Aeschines liked to represent Demosthenes as a godless fellow, and it is not perhaps without significance that the latter never directly replied to such attacks, or indirectly did anything to impair their force.

During the violent revolutions that took place in Hellas under Alexander the Great and his successors, and the instability of social and political conditions consequent thereon, the Tyche-religion received a fresh impetus. With one stroke Hellas was flung into world politics. Everything grew to colossal proportions in comparison with earlier conditions. The small Hellenic city-states that had hitherto been each for itself a world shrank into nothing. It is as if the old gods could not keep pace with this violent process of expansion. Men felt a craving for a wider and more comprehensive religious concept to answer to the changed conditions, and such an idea was found in the idea of Tyche. Thoughtful men, such as Demetrius of Phalerum, wrote whole books about it ; states built temples to

Tyche ; in private religion also it played a great part. No one reflected much on the relation of Tyche to the old gods. It must be remembered that Tyche is a real layman's notion, and that Hellenistic philosophy regarded it as its task precisely to render man independent of the whims of fate. Sometimes, however, we find a positive statement of the view that Tyche ruled over the gods also. It is characteristic of the state of affairs ; men did not want to relinquish the old gods, but could not any longer allow them the leading place.

If we return for a moment to Polybius, we shall find that his conception of Tyche strikingly illustrates the distance between him and Thucydides. In the introduction to his work, on its first page, he points out that the universally acknowledged task of historical writing is partly to educate people for political activities, partly to teach them to bear the vicissitudes of fortune with fortitude by reminding them of the lot of others. And subsequently, when he passes on to his main theme, the foundation of the Roman world-empire, after having explained the plan of his work, he says : " So far then our plan. But the *co-operation of fortune* is still needed if my life is to be long enough for me to accomplish my purpose." An earlier—or a later—author would here either have left the higher powers out of the game altogether or would have used an expression showing more submission to the gods of the popular faith.

In a later author, Pliny the Elder, we again find a characteristic utterance throwing light upon the significance of the Tyche-religion. After a very free-thinking survey of the popular notions regarding the gods, Pliny says : " As an intermediate position between these two views (that there is a divine providence and that there is none) men have themselves invented another divine power, in order that speculation about the deity might become still more uncertain. Throughout the world, in every place, at every hour of the day, Fortune alone is invoked and named by every mouth ; she alone is accused, she bears the guilt of everything ; of her only do we think, to her is all praise, to her all blame. And she is worshipped with railing words—she is deemed inconstant, by many even blind ; she is fickle, unstable, uncertain, changeable ; giving her favours to the unworthy. To her is imputed every loss, every gain ; in all the accounts of life she alone fills up both the debit and the credit side, and we are so subject to chance that Chance itself becomes our god, and again proves the incertitude of the deity." Even if a great deal of this may be put down to rhetoric, by which Pliny was easily carried away, the solid fact itself remains that he felt justified in speaking as if Dame Fortune had dethroned all the old gods.

That this view of life must have persisted very tenaciously even down to a time when a strong reaction in the direction of positive religious feeling had set in, is proved by the romances of the time. The novels of the ancients were in general poor productions. Most of them are made after the recipe of a little misfortune in each chapter and great happiness in the last. The two lovers meet, fall in love, part, and suffer a series of troubles individually until they are finally united. The power that governs their fates and shapes everything according to this pattern is regularly Tyche, never the gods. The testimony of the novels is of special significance because they were read by the general mass of the educated classes, not by the select who had philosophy to guide them.

Another testimony to the weakening of popular faith in the Hellenistic age is the decay of the institution of the Oracle. This, also, is of early date ; as early as the fifth and fourth century we hear much less of the interference of the oracles in political matters than in earlier times. The most important of them all, the Delphic Oracle, was dealt a terrible blow in the Holy War (356–346 B.C.), when the Phocians seized it and used the treasures which had been accumulated in it during centuries to hire mercenaries and carry on war. Such proceedings would assuredly have been impossible a century earlier ; no soldiers could have been hired with money acquired in such a way, or, if they could have been procured, all Hellas would have risen in arms against the robbers of the Temple, whereas in the Holy War most of the states were indifferent, and several even sided with the Phocians. In the succeeding years, after Philip of Macedonia had put an end to the Phocian scandal, the Oracle was in reality in his hands—it was during this period that Demosthenes stigmatised it as the mouthpiece of Philip. In the succeeding centuries, too, it was dependent on the various rulers of Hellas and undoubtedly lost all public authority. During this period we hear very little of the oracles of Hellas until the time before and after the birth of Christ provides us with definite evidence of their complete decay.

Thus Strabo, who wrote during the reign of Augustus, says that the ancients attached more importance to divination generally and oracles more particularly, whereas people in his day were quite indifferent to these things. He gives as the reason that the Romans were content to use the Sibylline books and their own system of divination. His remark is made *a propos* of the Oracle in Libya, which was formerly in great repute, but was almost extinct in his time. He is undoubtedly correct as to the fact, but the decline of the oracular system cannot be explained by the indifference of the Romans. Plutarch, in a monograph on the discontinuance of the oracles, furnishes us with more detailed information. From this it appears that not only the Oracle of Ammon but also the numerous oracles of Boeotia had ceased to exist, with one exception, while even for the Oracle at Delphi, which had formerly employed three priestesses, a single one amply sufficed. We also note the remark that the questions submitted to the Oracle were mostly unworthy or of no importance.

The want of consideration sometimes shown to sacred places and things during the wars of the Hellenistic period may no doubt also be regarded as the result of a weakening of interest in the old gods. We have detailed information on this point from the war between Philip of Macedonia and the Aetolians in 220–217 B.C. The Aetolians began by destroying the temples at Dium and Dodona, whereupon Philip retaliated by totally wrecking the federal sanctuary of the Aetolians at Thermon. Of Philip's admiral Dicaearchus we are told by Polybius that wherever he landed he erected altars to " godlessness and lawlessness " and offered up sacrifice on them. Judging by the way he was hated, his practice must have answered to his theory.

One more phenomenon must be mentioned in this context, though it falls outside the limits within which we have hitherto moved, and though its connexion with free-thought and religious enlightenment will no doubt, on closer examination, prove disputable. This is the decay of the established worship of the Roman State in the later years of the Republic.

In the preceding pages there has been no occasion to include conditions in Rome in our investigation, simply because nothing has come down to us about atheism in the earlier days of Rome, and we may presume that it did not exist. Of any religious thought at Rome corresponding to that of the Greeks we hear nothing, nor did the Romans produce any philosophy. Whatever knowledge of philosophy there was at Rome was simply borrowed from the Greeks. The Greek influence was not seriously felt until the second century B.C., even though as early as about the middle of the third century the Romans, through the performance of plays translated from the Greek, made acquaintance with Greek dramatic poetry and the religious thought contained therein. Neither the latter, nor the heresies of the philosophers, seem to have made any deep impression upon them. Ennius, their most important poet of the second century, was no doubt strongly influenced by Greek free-thinking, but this was evidently an isolated phenomenon. Also, by birth Ennius was not a native of Rome but half a Greek. The testimony of Polybius (from the close of the second century) to Roman religious conservatism is emphatic enough. Its causes are doubtless of a complex nature, but as one of them the peculiar character of the Roman religion itself stands out prominently. However much it resembled Greek religion in externals—a resemblance which was strengthened by numerous loans both of religious rites and of deities—it is decidedly distinct from it in being restricted still more to cultus and, above all, in being entirely devoid of mythology. The Roman gods were powers about the rites of whose worship the most accurate details were known or could be ascertained if need were, but they had little personality, and about their personal relations people knew little and cared less. This was, aesthetically, a great defect. The Roman gods afforded no good theme for poetry and art, and when they were to be used as such they were invariably replaced by loans from the Greeks. But, as in the face of Greek free-thought and Greek criticism of religion, they had the advantage that the vital point for attack was lacking. All the objectionable tales of the exploits of the gods and the associated ideas about their nature which had prompted the Greek attack on the popular faith simply did not exist in Roman religion. On the other hand, its rites were in many points more primitive than the Greek ones, but Greek philosophy had been very reserved in its criticism of ritual. We may thus no doubt take it for granted, though we have no direct evidence to that effect, that even Romans with a Greek education long regarded the Greek criticism of religion as something foreign which was none of their concern.

That a time came when all this was changed ; that towards the end of the Republic great scepticism concerning the established religion of Rome was found among the upper classes, is beyond doubt, and we shall subsequently find occasion to consider this more closely. In this connexion another circumstance demands attention, one which, moreover, has by some been associated with Greek influence among the upper classes, namely, the decay of the established worship of the Roman State during the last years of the Republic. Of the actual facts there can hardly be any doubt, though we know very little about them. The decisive symptoms are : that Augustus, after having taken over the government, had to repair some eighty dilapidated temples in Rome and reinstitute a series of religious rites and priesthoods which had ceased to function. Among them was one of the most important, that of the priest of Jupiter, an office which had been vacant for more than seventy-five years (87–11 B.C.), because it excluded the holder from a political career. Further, that complaints were made of private persons encroaching on places that were reserved for religious worship ; and that Varro, when writing his great work on the Roman religion, in many cases was unable to discover what god was the object of an existing cult ; and generally, according to his own statement he wrote his work, among other things, in order to save great portions of the old Roman religion from falling into utter oblivion on account of the indifference of the Romans themselves. It is obvious that such a state of affairs would have been impossible in a community where the traditional religion was a living power, not only formally acknowledged by everybody, but felt to be a necessary of life, the spiritual daily bread, as it were, of the nation.

To hold, however, that the main cause of the decay of the established religion of Rome was the invasion of Greek culture, together with the fact that the members of the Roman aristocracy, from whom the priests were recruited and who superintended the cult, had become indifferent to the traditional religion through this influence, this, I think, is to go altogether astray. We may take it for granted that the governing classes in Rome would not have ventured to let the cult decay if there had been any serious interest in it among the masses of the population; and it is equally certain that Greek philosophy and religious criticism did not penetrate to these masses. When they became indifferent to the national religion, this was due to causes that had nothing to do with free-thought. The old Roman religion was adapted for a small, narrow and homogeneous community whose main constituent and real core consisted of the farmers, large and small, and minor artisans. In the last centuries of the Republic the social development had occasioned the complete decay of the Roman peasantry, and the free artisans had fared little better. In the place

8

of the old Rome had arisen the capital of an empire, inhabited by a population of a million and of extraordinarily mixed composition. Not only did this population comprise a number of immigrant foreigners, but, in consequence of the peculiar Roman rule that every slave on being set free attained citizenship, a large percentage of the citizens must of necessity have been of foreign origin. Only certain portions of the Roman religion, more especially the cult of the great central deities of the State religion, can have kept pace with these changed conditions; the remainder had in reality lost all hold on Roman society as it had developed in process of time, and was only kept alive by force of habit. To this must be added the peculiar Roman mixture of mobility and conservatism in religious matters. The Roman superstition and uncertainty in regard to the gods led on the one hand to a continual setting up of new cults and new sanctuaries, and on the other hand to a fear of letting any of the old cults die out. In consequence thereof a great deal of dead and worthless ritual material must have accumulated in Rome in the course of centuries, and was of course in the way during the rapid development of the city in the last century of the Republic. Things must gradually have come to such a pass that a thorough reform, above all a reduction, of the whole cult had become a necessity. To introduce such a reform the republican government was just as unsuited as it was to carry out all the other tasks imposed by the development of the empire and the capital at that time. On this point, however, it must not be forgotten that the governing class not only lacked ability, for political reasons, to carry out serious reforms, but also the will to do so, on account of religious indifference, and so let things go altogether to the bad. The consequence was anarchy, in this as in all other spheres at that time ; but at the same time the tendency towards the only sensible issue, a restriction of the old Roman State-cult, is plainly evident. The simultaneous strong infusion of foreign religions was unavoidable in the mixed population of the capital. That these influences also affected the lower classes of the citizens is at any rate a proof that they were not indifferent to religion.

In its main outlines this is all the information that I have been able to glean about the general decline of the belief in the gods during the Hellenistic period. Judging from such information we should expect to find strong tendencies to atheism in the philosophy of the period. These anticipations are, however, doomed to disappointment. The ruling philosophical schools on the whole preserved a friendly attitude towards the gods of the popular faith and especially towards their worship, although they only accepted the existing religion with strict reservation.

Most characteristic but least consistent and original was the attitude of the Stoic school. The Stoics were pantheists. Their deity was a substance which they designated as fire, but which, it must be admitted, differed greatly from fire as an element. It permeated the entire world. It had produced the world out of itself, and it absorbed it again, and this process was repeated to eternity. The divine fire was also reason, and as such the cause of the harmony of the world-order. What of conscious reason was found in the world was part of the divine reason.

Though in this scheme of things there was in the abstract plenty of room for the gods of popular belief, nevertheless the Stoics did not in reality acknowledge them. In principle their standpoint was the same as Aristotle's. They supposed the heavenly bodies to be divine, but all the rest, namely, the anthropomorphic gods, were nothing to them.

In their explanation of the origin of the gods they went beyond Aristotle, but their doctrine was not always the same on this point. The earlier Stoics regarded mythology and all theology as human inventions, but not arbitrary inventions. Mythology, they thought, should be understood allegorically; it was the naïve expression partly of a correct conception of Nature, partly of ethical and metaphysical truths. Strictly speaking, men had always been Stoics, though in an imperfect way. This point of view was elaborated in detail by the first Stoics, who took their stand partly on the earlier naturalism which had already broken the ground in this direction, and partly on sophistic, so that they even brought into vogue again the theory of Prodicus, that the gods were a hypostasis of the benefits of civilisation. Such a standpoint could not of course be maintained without arbitrariness and absurdities which exposed it to embarrassing criticism. This seems to have been the reason why the later Stoics, and expecially Poseidonius, took another road. They adopted the doctrine of

Xenocrates with regard to demons and developed it in fantastic forms. The earlier method was not, however, given up, and at the time of Cicero we find both views represented in the doctrine of the school.

Such is the appearance of the theory. In both its forms it is evidently an attempt to meet popular belief half-way from a standpoint which is really beyond it. This tendency is seen even more plainly in the practice of the Stoics. They recognised public worship and insisted on its advantages ; in their moral reflections they employed the gods as ideals in the Socratic manner, regardless of the fact that in their theory they did not really allow for gods who were ideal men ; nay, they even went the length of giving to their philosophical deity, the " universal reason," the name of Zeus by preference, though it had nothing but the name in common with the Olympian ruler of gods and men. This pervading ambiguity brought much well-deserved reproof on the Stoics even in ancient times; but, however unattractive it may seem to us, it is of significance as a manifestation of the great hold popular belief continued to have even on the minds of the upper classes, for it was to these that the Stoics appealed.

Far more original and consistent is the Epicurean attitude towards the popular faith. Epicurus unreservedly acknowledged its foundation, i.e. the existence of anthropomorphic beings of a higher order than man. His gods had human shape but they were eternal and blessed. In the latter definition was included, according to the ethical ideal of Epicurus, the idea that the gods were free from every care, including taking an interest in nature or in human affairs. They were entirely outside the world, a fact to which Epicurus gave expression by placing them in the empty spaces between the infinite number of spherical worlds which he assumed. There his gods lived in bliss like ideal Epicureans. Lucretius, the only poet of this school, extolled them in splendid verse whose motif he borrowed from Homer's description of Olympus. In this way Epicurus also managed to uphold public worship itself. It could not, of course, have any practical aim, but it was justified as an expression of the respect man owed to beings whose existence expressed the human ideal.

The reasons why Epicurus assumed this attitude towards popular belief are simple enough. He maintained that the evidence of sensual perception was the basis of all knowledge, and he thought that the senses (through dreams) gave evidence of the existence of the gods. And in the popular ideas of the bliss of the gods he found his ethical ideal directly confirmed. As regards their eternity the case was more difficult. The basis of his system was the theory that everything was made of atoms and that only the atoms as such, not the bodies composed of the atoms, were eternal. He conceived the gods, too, as made of atoms, nevertheless he held that they were eternal. Any rational explanation of this postulate is not possible on Epicurus's hypotheses, and the criticism of his theology was therefore especially directed against this point.

Epicurus was the Greek philosopher who most consistently took the course of emphasising the popular dogma of the perfection of the gods in order to preserve the popular notions about them. And he was the philosopher to whom this would seem the most obvious course, because his ethical ideal— quietism—agreed with the oldest popular ideal of divine existence. In this way Epicureanism became the most orthodox of all Greek philosophical schools. If nevertheless Epicurus did not escape the charge of atheism the sole reason is that his whole theology was denounced off-hand as hypocrisy. It was assumed to be set up by him only to shield himself against a charge of impiety, not to be his actual belief. This accusation is now universally acknowledged to be unjustified, and the Epicureans had no difficulty in rebutting it with interest. They took special delight in pointing out that the theology of the other schools was much more remote from popular belief than theirs, nay, in spite of recognition of the existing religion, was in truth fundamentally at variance with it. But in reality their own was in no better case : gods who did not trouble in the least about human affairs were beings for whom popular belief had no use. It made no difference that Epicurus's definition of the nature of the gods was the direct outcome of a fundamental doctrine of popular belief. Popular religion will not tolerate pedantry.

In this connexion we cannot well pass over a third philosophical school which played no inconspicuous rôle in the latter half of our period, namely, Scepticism. The Sceptic philosophy as such dates from Socrates, from whom the so-called Megarian school took its origin, but it did not reach its greatest importance until the second century, when the

Academic school became Sceptic.   It was especially
the famous philosopher Carneades, a brilliant
master of logic and dialectic, who made a success
by his searching negative criticism of the doctrines
of the other philosophical schools (the Dogmatics).
For such criticism the theology of the philosophers
was a grateful subject, and Carneades did not spare
it.   Here as in all the investigations of the Sceptics
the theoretical result was that no scientific certainty
could be attained : it was equally wrong to assert
or to deny the existence of the gods.   But in practice
the attitude of the Sceptics was quite different.
Just as they behaved like other people, acting upon
their immediate impressions and experience, though
they did not believe that anything could be scientifically proved, *e.g.* not even the reality of the world
of the senses, so also did they acknowledge the
existing cult and lived generally like good heathens.
Characteristic though Scepticism be of a period of
Greek spiritual life in which Greek thought lost its
belief in itself, it was, however, very far from sup-
porting atheism.   On the contrary, according to the
correct Sceptic doctrine atheism was a dogmatic
contention which theoretically was as objectionable
as its antithesis, and in practice was to be utterly
discountenanced.

A more radical standpoint than this as regards
the gods of the popular faith is not found during
the Hellenistic period except among the less noted
schools, and in the beginning of the period. We
have already mentioned such thinkers as Strato,
Theodorus, and Stilpo ; chronologically they belong to the Hellenistic Age, but in virtue of their

connexion with the Socratic philosophy they were dealt with in the last chapter. A definite polemical attitude towards the popular faith is also a characteristic of the Cynic school, hence, though our information is very meagre, we must speak of it a little more fully.

The Cynics continued the tendency of Antisthenes, but the school comparatively soon lost its importance. After the third century we hear no more about the Cynics until they crop up again about the year A.D. 100. But in the fourth and third centuries the school had important representatives. The most famous is Diogenes ; his life, to be sure, is entangled in such a web of legend that it is difficult to arrive at a true picture of his personality. Of his attitude towards popular belief we know one thing, that he did not take part in the worship of the gods. This was a general principle of the Cynics ; their argument was that the gods were " in need of nothing " (cf. above, pp. 60 and 41). If we find him accused of atheism, in an anecdote of very doubtful value, it may, if there is anything in it, be due to his rejection of worship. Of one of his successors, however, Bion of Borysthenes, we have authentic information that he denied the existence of the gods, with the edifying legend attached that he was converted before his death. But we also hear of Bion that he was a disciple of the atheist Theodorus, and other facts go to suggest that Bion united Cynic and Hedonistic principles in his mode of life—a compromise that was not so unlikely as might be supposed. Bion's attitude cannot therefore be taken as typical of Cynicism. Another

Cynic of about the same period (the beginning of the third century) was Menippus of Gadara (in northern Palestine). He wrote tales and dialogues in a mixture of prose and verse. The contents were satirical, the satire being directed against the contemporary philosophers and their doctrines, and against the popular notions of the gods. Menippus availed himself partly of the old criticism of mythology and partly of the philosophical attacks on the popular conception of the gods. The only novelty was the facetious form in which he concealed the sting of serious criticism. It is impossible to decide whether he positively denied the existence of the gods, but his satire on the popular notions and its success among his contemporaries at least testifies to the weakening of the popular faith among the educated classes. In Hellas itself he seems to have gone out of fashion very early ; but the Romans took him up again ; Varro and Seneca imitated him, and Lucian made his name famous again in the Greek world in the second century after Christ. It is chiefly due to Lucian that we can form an idea of Menippus's literary work, hence we shall return to Cynic satire in our chapter on the age of the Roman Empire.

During our survey of Greek philosophical thought in the Hellenistic period we have only met with a few cases of atheism in the strict sense, and they all occur about and immediately after 300, though there does not seem to be any internal connexion between them. About the same time there appeared a writer, outside the circle of philosophers, who is regularly listed among the *atheoi*, and who has given a name to a peculiar theory about the origin of the idea of the gods, namely, Euhemerus. He is said to have travelled extensively in the service of King Cassander of Macedonia. At any rate he published his theological views in the shape of a book of travel which was, however, wholly fiction. He relates how he came to an island, Panchaia, in the Indian Ocean, and in a temple there found a lengthy inscription in which Uranos, Kronos, Zeus and other gods recorded their exploits. The substance of the tale was that these gods had once been men, great kings and rulers, who had bestowed on their peoples all sorts of improvements in civilisation and had thus got themselves worshipped as gods. It appears from the accounts that Euhemerus supposed the heavenly bodies to be real and eternal gods—he thought that Uranos had first taught men to worship them ; further, as his theory is generally understood, it must be assumed that in his opinion the other gods had ceased to exist as such after their death. This accords with the fact that Euhemerus was generally characterised as an atheist.

The theory that the gods were at first men was not originated by Euhemerus, though it takes its name (Euhemerism) from him. The theory had some support in the popular faith which recognised gods (Heracles, Asclepius) who had lived as men on earth ; and the opinion which was fundamental to Greek religion, that the gods had *come into existence*, and had not existed from eternity, would favour this theory. Moreover, Euhemerus had had an immediate precursor in the slightly earlier

Hecataeus of Abdera, who had set forth a similar theory, with the difference, however, that he took the view that all excellent men became real gods. But Euhemerus's theory appeared just at the right moment and fell on fertile soil. Alexander the Great and his successors had adopted the Oriental policy by which the ruler was worshipped as a god, and were supported in this by a tendency which had already made itself felt occasionally among the Greeks in the East. Euhemerus only inverted matters—if the rulers were gods, it was an obvious inference that the gods were rulers. No wonder that his theory gained a large following. Its great influence is seen from numerous similar attempts in the Hellenistic world. At Rome, in the second century, Ennius translated his works into Latin, and as late as the time of Augustus an author such as Diodorus, in his popular history of the world, served up Euhemerism as the best scientific explanation of the origin of religion. It is characteristic, too, that both Jews and Christians, in their attacks on Paganism, reckoned with Euhemerism as a well-established theory. As every one knows, it has survived to our day; Carlyle, I suppose, being its last prominent exponent.

It is characteristic of Euhemerism in its most radical form that it assumed that the gods of polytheism did not exist; so far it is atheism. But it is no less characteristic that it made the concession to popular belief that its gods had once existed. Hereby it takes its place, in spite of its greater radicalism, on the same plane with most other ancient theories about the origin of men's notions about the gods.   The gods of popular belief could not survive in the light of ancient thought, which in its essence was free-thought, not tied down by dogmas.   But the philosophers of old could not but believe that a psychological fact of such enormous dimensions as ancient polytheism must have something answering to it in the objective world.   Ancient philosophy never got clear of this dilemma ; hence Plato's open recognition of the absurdity ; hence Aristotle's delight at being able to meet the popular faith half-way in his assumption of the divinity of the heavenly bodies ; hence Xeno-crates's demons, the allegories of the Stoics, the ideal Epicureans of Epicurus, Euhemerus's early benefactors of mankind.   And we may say that the more the Greeks got to know of the world about them the more they were confirmed in their view, for in the varied multiplicity of polytheism they found the same principle everywhere, the same belief in a multitude of beings of a higher order than man.

Euhemerus's theory is no doubt the last serious attempt in the old pagan world to give an explana-tion of the popular faith which may be called genuine atheism.   We will not, however, leave the Hellenistic period without casting a glance at some personalities about whom we have information enough to form an idea at first hand of their re-ligious standpoint, and whose attitude towards popular belief at any rate comes very near to atheism pure and simple.

One of them is Polybius.   In the above-cited passage referring to the decline of the popular faith in the Hellenistic period, Polybius also gives his own

theory of the origin of men's notions regarding the
gods. It is not new. It is the theory known from
the Critias fragment, what may be called the political theory. In the fragment it appears as atheism
pure and simple, and it seems obvious to understand
it in the same way in Polybius. That he shows a
leaning towards Euhemerism in another passage
where he speaks about the origin of religious ideas, is
in itself not against this—the two theories are closely
related and might very well be combined. But we
have a series of passages in which Polybius expressed
himself in a way that seems quite irreconcilable with
a purely atheistic standpoint. He expressly acknowledged divination and worship as justified ; in
several places he refers to disasters that have
befallen individuals or a whole people as being sent
by the gods, or even as a punishment for impiety ;
and towards the close of his work he actually, in
marked contrast to the tone of its beginning, offers
up a prayer to the gods to grant him a happy ending
to his long life. It would seem as if Polybius at a
certain period of his life came under the influence of
Stoicism and in consequence greatly modified his
earlier views. That these were of an atheistic
character seems, however, beyond doubt, and that
is the decisive point in this connexion.

Cicero's philosophical standpoint was that of an
Academic, *i.e.* a Sceptic. But—in accord, for the
rest, with the doctrines of the school just at this
period—he employed his liberty as a Sceptic to
favour such philosophical doctrines as seemed to
him more reasonable than others, regardless of the
school from which they were derived. In his

philosophy of religion he was more especially a Stoic. He himself expressly insisted on this point of view in the closing words of his work on the *Nature of the Gods*. As he was not, and made no pretence of being, a philosopher, his philosophical expositions have no importance for us ; they are throughout second-hand, mostly mere translations from Greek sources. That we have employed them in the fore-going pages to throw light on the theology of the earlier, more especially the Hellenistic, philosophy, goes without saying. But his personal religious standpoint is not without interest.

As orator and statesman Cicero took his stand wholly on the side of the established Roman religion, operating with the " immortal gods," with Jupiter Optimus Maximus, etc., at his convenience. In his works on the *State* and the *Laws* he adheres decidedly to the established religion. But all this is mere politics. Personally Cicero had no religion other than philosophy. Philosophy was his consolation in adversity, or he attempted to make it so, for the result was often indifferent ; and he looked to philosophy to guide him in ethical questions. We never find any indication in his writings that the gods of popular belief meant anything to him in these respects. And what is more—he assumed this off-hand to be the standpoint of everybody else, and evidently he was justified. A great number of letters from him to his circle, and not a few from his friends and acquaintances to him, have been pre-served ; and in his philosophical writings he often introduces contemporary Romans as characters in the dialogue. But in all this literature there is never the faintest indication that a Roman of the better class entertained, or could even be supposed to entertain, an orthodox view with regard to the State religion. To Cicero and his circle the popular faith did not exist as an element of their personal religion.

Such a standpoint is of course, practically speaking, atheism, and in this sense atheism was widely spread among the higher classes of the Graeco-Roman society about the time of the birth of Christ. But from this to theoretical atheism there is still a good step. Cicero himself affords an amusing example of how easily people, who have apparently quite emancipated themselves from the official religion of their community, may backslide. When his beloved daughter Tullia died in the year 45 B.C., it became evident that Cicero, in the first violence of his grief, which was the more overwhelming because he was excluded from political activity during Cæsar's dictatorship, could not console himself with philosophy alone. He wanted something more tangible to take hold on, and so he hit upon the idea of having Tullia exalted among the gods. He thought of building a temple and instituting a cult in her honour. He moved heaven and earth to arrange the matter, sought to buy ground in a prominent place in Rome, and was willing to make the greatest pecuniary sacrifices to get a conspicuous result. Nothing came of it all, however ; Cicero's friends, who were to help him to put the matter through, were perhaps hardly so eager as he ; time assuaged his own grief, and finally he contented himself with publishing a consolatory epistle written

by himself, or, correctly speaking, translated from a
famous Greek work and adapted to the occasion.
So far he ended where he should, *i.e.* in philosophy ;
but the little incident is significant, not least
because it shows what practical ends Euhemerism
could be brought to serve and how doubtful was
its atheistic character after all.   For not only was
the contemplated apotheosis of Tullia in itself a
Euhemeristic idea, but Cicero also expressly defended it with Euhemeristic arguments, though
speaking as if the departed who were worshipped as
gods really had become gods.

The attitude of Cicero and his contemporaries
towards popular belief was still the general attitude
in the first days of the Empire.   It was of no avail
that Augustus re-established the decayed State cult
in all its splendour and variety, or that the poets
during his reign, when they wished to express themselves in harmony with the spirit of the new régime,
directly or indirectly extolled the revived orthodoxy.
Wherever we find personal religious feeling expressed
by men of that time, in the Epistles of Horace, in
Virgil's posthumous minor poems or in such passages in his greater works where he expresses his own
ideals, it is philosophy that is predominant and the
official religion ignored.   Virgil was an Epicurean ;
Horace an Eclectic, now an Epicurean, then a Stoic ;
Augustus had a domestic philosopher.   Ovid employed his genius in writing travesties of the old
mythology while at the same time he composed a
poem, serious for him, on the Roman cult ; and when
disaster befell him and he was cast out from the
society of the capital, which was the breath of life

9

to him, he was abandoned not only by men, but also by the gods—he had not even a philosophy with which to console himself. It is only in inferior writers such as Valerius Maximus, who wrote a work on great deeds—good and evil—under Tiberius, that we find a different spirit.

Direct utterances about men's relationship to the gods, from which conclusions can be drawn, are seldom met with during this period. The whole question was so remote from the thoughts of these people that they never mentioned it except when they assumed an orthodox air for political or aesthetic reasons. Still, here and there we come across something. One of the most significant pronouncements is that of Pliny the Elder, from whom we quoted the passage about the worship of Fortune. Pliny opens his scientific encyclopedia by explaining the structure of the universe in its broad features ; this he does on the lines of the physics of the Stoics, hence he designates the universe as God. Next comes a survey of special theology. It is introduced as follows : " I therefore deem it a sign of human weakness to ask about the shape and form of God. Whoever God is, if any other god (than the universe) exists at all, and in whatever part of the world he is, he is all perception, all sight, all hearing, all soul, all reason, all self." The popular notions of the gods are then reviewed, in the most supercilious tone, and their absurdities pointed out. A polite bow is made to the worship of the Emperors and its motives, the rest is little but persiflage. Not even Providence, which was recognised by the Stoics, is acknowledged by

Pliny. The conclusion is like the beginning : " To imperfect human nature it is a special consolation that God also is not omnipotent (he can neither put himself to death, even if he would, though he has given man that power and it is his choicest gift in this punishment which is life ; nor can he give immortality to mortals or call the dead to life ; nor can he bring it to pass that those who have lived have not lived, or that he who has held honourable offices did not hold them) ; and that he has no other power over the past than that of oblivion ; and that (in order that we may also give a jesting proof of our partnership with God) he cannot bring it about that twice ten is not twenty, and more of the same sort—by all which the power of Nature is clearly revealed, and that it is this we call God."

An opinion like that expressed here must without doubt be designated as atheism, even though it is nothing but the Stoic pantheism logically carried out. As we have said before, we rarely meet it so directly expressed, but there can hardly be any doubt that even in the time of Pliny it was quite common in Rome. At this point, then, had the educated classes of the ancient world arrived under the influence of Hellenistic philosophy.

CHAPTER VII

THOUGH the foundation of the Empire in many ways inaugurated a new era for the antique world, it is, of course, impossible, in an inquiry which is not confined to political history in the narrowest sense of the word, to operate with anything but the loosest chronological divisions. Accordingly in the last chapter we had to include phenomena from the early days of the Empire in order not to separate things which naturally belonged together. From the point of view of religious history the dividing line cannot possibly be drawn at the Emperor Augustus, in spite of his restoration of worship and the orthodox reaction in the official Augustan poetry, but rather at about the beginning of the second century. The enthusiasm of the Augustan Age for the good old times was never much more than affectation. It quickly evaporated when the promised millennium was not forthcoming, and was replaced by a reserve which developed into cynicism—but, be it understood, in the upper circles of the capital only. In the empire at large the development took its natural tranquil course, unaffected by the manner in which the old Roman nobility was effacing itself ; and this development did not tend towards atheism.

The reaction towards positive religious feeling,

which becomes clearly manifest in the second century after Christ, though the preparation for it is
undoubtedly of earlier date, is perhaps the most
remarkable phenomenon in the religious history of
antiquity. This is not the place to inquire into
its causes, which still remain largely unexplained ;
there is even no reason to enter more closely into its
outer manifestations, as the thing itself is doubted
by nobody. It is sufficient to mention as instances
authors like Suetonius, with his naïve belief in
miracles, and the rhetorician Aristides, with his
Asclepius-cult and general sanctimoniousness ; or
a minor figure such as Aelian, who wrote whole
books of a pronounced, nay even fanatical, devotion-
alism ; or within the sphere of philosophy movements like Neo-Pythagoreanism and Neo-Platonism,
both of which are as much in the nature of mystic
theology as attempts at a scientific explanation
of the universe. It is characteristic, too, that an
essentially anti-religious school like that of the
Epicureans actually dies out at this time. Under
these conditions our task in this chapter must be to
bring out the comparatively few and weak traces of
other currents which still made themselves felt.

Of the earlier philosophical schools Stoicism
flowered afresh in the second century ; the Emperor Marcus Aurelius himself was a prominent
adherent of the creed. This later Stoicism differs,
however, somewhat from the earlier. It limits the
scientific apparatus which the early Stoics had
operated with to a minimum, and is almost exclusively concerned with practical ethics on a
religious basis. Its religion is that of ordinary

Stoicism : Pantheism and belief in Providence. But, on the whole, it takes up a more sympathetic attitude towards popular religion than early Stoicism had done. Of the bitter criticism of the absurdities of the worship of the gods and of mythology which is still to be met with as late as Seneca, nothing remains. On the contrary, participation in public worship is still enjoined as being a duty ; nay, more : attacks on belief in the gods—in the plain popular sense of the word—are denounced as pernicious and reprehensible. Perhaps no clearer proof could be adduced of the revolution which had taken place in the attitude of the educated classes towards popular religion than this change of front on the part of Stoicism.

Contrary to this was the attitude of another school which was in vogue at the same time as the Stoic, namely, the Cynic. Between Cynicism and popular belief strained relations had existed since early times. It is true, the Cynics did not altogether deny the existence of the gods ; but they rejected worship on the ground that the gods were not in need of anything, and they denied categorically the majority of the popular ideas about the gods. For the latter were, in fact, popular and traditional, and the whole aim of the Cynics was to antagonise the current estimate of values. A characteristic instance of their manner is provided by this very period in the fragments of the work of Oenomaus. The work was entitled *The Swindlers Unmasked*, and it contained a violent attack on oracles. Its tone is exceedingly pungent. In the extant fragments Oenomaus addresses the god in

Delphi and overwhelms him with insults.   But we are expressly told—and one utterance of Oenomaus himself verifies it—that the attack was not really directed against the god, but against the men who gave oracles in his name.   In his opinion the whole thing was a priestly fraud—a view which otherwise was rather unfamiliar to the ancients, but played an important part later.   Incidentally there is a violent attack on idolatry.   The work is not without acuteness of thought and a certain coarse wit of the true Cynical kind ;   but it is entirely uncritical (oracles are used which are evidently inventions of later times) and of no great significance.   It is even difficult to avoid the impression that the author's aim is in some degree to create a sensation.   Cynics of that day were not strangers to that kind of thing. But it is at any rate a proof of the fact that there were at the time tendencies opposed to the religious reaction.

A more significant phenomenon of the same kind is to be found in the writings of Lucian.   Lucian was by education a rhetorician, by profession an itinerant lecturer and essayist.   At a certain stage of his life he became acquainted with the Cynic philosophy and for some time felt much attracted to it.   From that he evidently acquired a sincere contempt of the vulgar superstition which flourished in his time, even in circles of which one might have expected something better.   In writings which for the greater part belong to his later period, he pilloried individuals who traded (or seemed to trade) in the religious ferment of the time, as well as satirised superstition as such.   In this way he made an important contribution to the spiritual history of the age. But simultaneously he produced, for the entertainment of his public, a series of writings the aim of which is to make fun of the Olympian gods. In this work also he leant on the literature of the Cynics, but substituted for their grave and biting satire light causeries or slight dramatic sketches, in which his wit—for Lucian was really witty—had full scope. As an instance of his manner I shall quote a short passage from the dialogue *Timon*. It is Zeus who speaks ; he has given Hermes orders to send the god of wealth to Timon, who has wasted his fortune by his liberality and is now abandoned by his false friends. Then he goes on : " As to the flatterers you speak of and their ingratitude, I shall deal with them another time, and they will meet with their due punishment as soon as I have had my thunderbolt repaired. The two largest darts of it were broken and blunted the other day when I got in a rage and flung it at the sophist Anaxagoras, who was trying to make his disciples believe that we gods do not exist at all. However, I missed him, for Pericles held his hand over him, but the bolt struck the temple of the Dioscuri and set fire to it, and the bolt itself was nearly destroyed when it struck the rock." This sort of thing abounds in Lucian, even if it is not always equally amusing and to the point. Now there is nothing strange in the fact that a witty man for once should feel inclined to make game of the old mythology ; this might have happened almost at any time, once the critical spirit had been awakened. But that a man, and moreover an essayist, who had to live by the approval of his public, should make it his trade, as it were, and that at a time of vigorous religious reaction, seems more difficult to account for. Lucian's controversial pamphlets against superstition cannot be classed off-hand with his *Dialogues of the Gods*; the latter are of a quite different and far more harmless character. The fact is rather that mythology at this time was fair game. It was cut off from its connexion with religion—a connexion which in historical times was never very intimate and was now entirely severed. This had been brought about in part by centuries of criticism of the most varied kind, in part precisely as a result of the religious reaction which had now set in. If people turned during this time to the old gods—who, however, had been considerably contaminated with new elements—it was because they had nothing else to turn to ; but what they now looked for was something quite different from the old religion. The powerful tradition which had bound members of each small community—we should say, of each township—to its familiar gods, with all that belonged to them, was now in process of dissolution ; in the larger cities of the world-empire with their mixed populations it had entirely disappeared. Religion was no longer primarily a concern of society ; it was a personal matter. In the face of the enormous selection of gods which ancient paganism came gradually to proffer, the individual was free to choose, as individual or as a member of a communion based upon religious, not political, sympathy. Under these circumstances the existence of the gods and their power and will to help their worshippers was the only thing of interest ; all the old tales about them were more than ever myths of no religious value.   On closer inspection Lucian indeed proves to have exercised a certain selection in his satire. Gods like Asclepius and Serapis, who were popular in his day, he prefers to say nothing about ; and even with a phenomenon like Christianity he deals cautiously ; he sticks to the old Olympian gods. Thus his derision of these constitutes an indirect proof that they had gone out of vogue, and his forbearance on other points is a proof of the power of the current religion over contemporary minds.   As to ascribing any deeper religious conviction to Lucian— were it even of a purely negative kind—that is, in view of the whole character of his work, out of the question.   To be sure, his polemical pamphlets against superstition show clearly, like those of Oenomaus, that the religious reaction did not run its course without criticism from certain sides ; but even here it is significant that the criticism comes from a professional jester and not from a serious religious thinker.

A few words remain to be said about the two monotheistic religions which in the days of the Roman Empire came to play a great, one of them indeed a decisive, part. I have already referred to pagan society's attitude towards Judaism and Christianity, and pointed out that the adherents of both were designated and treated as atheists—the Jews only occasionally and with certain reservations, the Christians nearly always and unconditionally. The question here is, how far this designation was justified according to the definition of atheism which is the basis of our inquiry.

In the preceding pages we have several times referred to the fact that the real enemy of Polytheism
is not the philosophical theology, which generally
tends more or less towards Pantheism, but Monotheism.   It is in keeping with this that the Jews and
the Christians in practice are downright deniers of
the pagan gods : they would not worship them ;
whereas the Greek philosophers as a rule respected
worship, however far they went in their criticism of
men's ideas of the gods.   We shall not dwell here on
this aspect of the matter ; we are concerned with
the theory only.   Detailed expositions of it occur
in numerous writings, from the passages in the Old
Testament where heathenism is attacked, to the
defences of Christianity by the latest Fathers of the
Church.

The original Jewish view, according to which the
heathen gods are real beings just as much as the
God of the Jews themselves—only Jews must not
worship them—is in the later portions of the Old
Testament superseded by the view that the gods are
only images made of wood, stone or metal, and in-
capable of doing either good or evil.   This point of
view is taken over by later Jewish authors and
completely dominates them.   In those acquainted
with Greek thought it is combined with Euhemeristic ideas : the images represent dead men.   The
theory that the gods are really natural objects—
elements or heavenly bodies—is occasionally taken
into account too.   Alongside of these opinions there
appears also the view that the pagan gods are evil
spirits (demons).   It is already found in a few places
in the Old Testament, and after that sporadically

and quite incidentally in later Jewish writings ; in one place it is combined with the Old Testament's account of the fallen angels. The demon-theory is not an instrument of Jewish apologetics proper, not even of Philo, though he has a complete demonology and can hardly have been ignorant of the Platonic-Stoic doctrine of demons.

Apart from the few and, as it were, incidental utterances concerning demons, the Jewish view of the pagan gods impresses one as decidedly atheistic. The god is identical with the idol, and the idol is a dead object, the work of men's hands, or the god is identical with a natural object, made by God to be sure, but without soul or, at any rate, without divinity. It is remarkable that no Jewish controversialist seriously envisaged the problem of the real view of the gods embodied in the popular belief of the ancients, namely, that they are personal beings of a higher order than man. It is inconceivable that men like Philo, Josephus and the author of the Wisdom of Solomon should have been ignorant of it. I know nothing to account for this curious phenomenon ; and till some light has been thrown upon the matter, I should hesitate to assert that the Jewish conception of Polytheism was purely atheistic, however much appearance it may have of being so.

It was otherwise with Christian polemical writing. As early as St. Paul the demon-theory appears distinctly, though side by side with utterances of seemingly atheistic character. Other New Testament authors, too, designate the gods as demons. The subsequent apologists, excepting the earliest,

Aristides, lay the main stress on demonology, but include for the sake of completeness idolatry and the like, sometimes without caring about or trying to conciliate the contradictions. In the long run demonology is victorious; in St. Augustine, the foremost among Christian apologists, there is hardly any other point of view that counts.

To trace the Christian demonology in detail and give an account of its various aspects is outside the scope of this essay. Its origin is a twofold one, partly the Jewish demonology, which just at the commencement of our era had received a great impetus, partly the theory of the Greek philosophers, which we have characterised above when speaking of Xenocrates. The Christian doctrine regarding demons differs from the latter, especially by the fact that it does not acknowledge good demons; they were all evil. This was the indispensable basis for the interdict against the worship of demons; in its further development the Christians, following Jewish tradition, pointed to an origin in the fallen angels, and thus effected a connexion with the Old Testament. While they at the same time retained its angelology they had to distinguish good and evil beings intermediate between god and man; but they carefully avoided designating the angels as demons, and kept them distinct from the pagan gods, who were all demons and evil.

The application of demonology to the pagan worship caused certain difficulties in detail. To be sure, it was possible to identify a given pagan god with a certain demon, and this was often done; but it was impossible to identify the Pagans' conceptions of their gods with the Christians' conceptions of demons. The Pagans, in fact, ascribed to their gods not only demoniac (diabolical) but also divine qualities, which the Christians absolutely denied them. Consequently they had to recognise that pagan worship to a great extent rested on a delusion, on a misconception of the essential character of the gods which were worshipped. This view was corroborated by the dogma of the fallen angels, which was altogether alien to paganism. By identifying them with the evil spirits of the Bible, demon-names were even obtained which differed from those of the pagan gods and, of course, were the correct ones ; were they not given in Holy Writ ? In general, the Christians, who possessed an authentic revelation of the matter, were of course much better informed about the nature of the pagan gods than the Pagans themselves, who were groping in the dark. Euhemerism, which plays a great part in the apologists, helped in the same direction : the supposition that the idols were originally men existed among the Pagans themselves, and it was too much in harmony with the tendency of the apologists to be left unemployed. It was reconciled with demon-ology by the supposition that the demons had assumed the masks of dead heroes ; they had be-guiled mankind to worship them in order to possess themselves of the sacrifices, which they always coveted, and by this deception to be able to rule and corrupt men. The Christians also could not avoid recognising that part of the pagan worship was worship of natural objects, in particular of the heavenly bodies ; and this error of worshipping the

" creation instead of the creator " was so obvious that the Christians were not inclined to resort to demonology for an explanation of this phenomenon, the less so as they could not identify the sun or the moon with a demon.   The conflict of these different points of view accounts for the peculiar vacillation in the Christian conception of paganism.   On one hand, we meet with crude conceptions, according to which the pagan gods are just like so many demons ; they are specially prominent when. pagan miracles and prophecies are to be explained.   On the other hand, there is a train of thought which carried to its logical conclusion would lead to conceiving paganism as a whole as a huge delusion of humanity, but a delusion caused indeed by supernatural agencies. This conclusion hardly presented itself to the early Church ; later, however, it was drawn and caused a not inconsiderable shifting in men's views and explanations of paganism.

Demonology is to such a degree the ruling point of view in Christian apologetics that it would be absurd to make a collection from these writings of utterances with an atheistic ring.   Such utterances are to be found in most of them ; they appear spontaneously, for instance, wherever idolatry is attacked.   But one cannot attach any importance to them when they appear in this connexion, not even in apologists in whose works the demon theory is lacking.   No Christian theologian in antiquity advanced, much less sustained, the view that the pagan gods were mere phantoms of human imagination without any corresponding reality.

Remarkable as this state of things may appear

to us moderns, it is really quite simple, nay even a matter of course, when regarded historically.   Christianity had from its very beginning a decidedly dualistic character. The contrast between this world and the world to come was identical with the contrast between the kingdom of the Devil and the kingdom of God. As soon as the new religion came into contact with paganism, the latter was necessarily regarded as belonging to the kingdom of the Devil ; thus the conception of the gods as demons was a foregone conclusion.   In the minds of the later apologists, who became acquainted with Greek philosophy, this conception received additional confirmation ; did it not indeed agree in the main with Platonic and Stoic theory ?   Details were added : the Christians could not deny the pagan miracles without throwing a doubt on their own, for miracles cannot be done away with at all except by a denial on principle ; neither could they explain paganism—that gigantic, millennial aberration of humanity—by merely human causes, much less lay the blame on God alone.   But ultimately all this rests on one and the same thing—the supernatural and dualistic hypothesis.   Consequently demonology is the kernel of the Christian conception of paganism : it is not merely a natural result of the hypotheses, it is the one and only correct expression of the way in which the new religion understood the old.

CHAPTER VIII

IN the preceding inquiry we took as our starting-point not the ancient conception of atheism but the modern view of the nature of the pagan gods. It proved that this view was, upon the whole, feebly represented during antiquity, and that it was another view (demonology) which was transmitted to later ages from the closing years of antiquity. The inquiry will therefore find its natural conclusion in a demonstration of the time and manner in which the conception handed down from antiquity of the nature of paganism was superseded and displaced by the modern view.

This question is, however, more difficult to answer than one would perhaps think. After ancient paganism had ceased to exist as a living religion, it had lost its practical interest, and theoretically the Middle Ages were occupied with quite other problems than the nature of paganism. At the revival of the study of ancient literature, during the Renaissance, people certainly again came into the most intimate contact with ancient religion itself, but systematic investigations of its nature do not seem to have been taken up in real earnest until after the middle of the sixteenth century. It is therefore difficult to ascertain in what light paganism was regarded during the thousand

years which had then passed since its final extinction.
From the seventeenth and eighteenth centuries, on
the other hand, the material is extraordinarily
plentiful, though but slightly investigated. Previous works in this field seem to be entirely wanting ;
at any rate it has not been possible for me to find
any collective treatment of the subject, nor even
any contributions worth mentioning towards the
solution of the numerous individual problems
which arise when we enter upon what might be
called " the history of the history of religion." [1]   In
this essay I must therefore restrict myself to a few
aphoristic remarks which may perhaps give occasion
for this subject, in itself not devoid of interest, to
receive more detailed treatment at some future time.

Milton, in the beginning of *Paradise Lost*, which
appeared in 1667, makes Satan assemble all his
angels for continued battle against God. Among
the demons there enumerated, ancient gods also
appear ; they are, then, plainly regarded as devils.
Now Milton was not only a poet, but also a sound
scholar and an orthodox theologian ; we may therefore rest assured that his conception of the pagan
gods was dogmatically correct and in accord with
the prevailing views of his time.   In him, therefore,
we have found a fixed point from which we can
look forwards and backwards ; as late as after
the middle of the seventeenth century the early
Christian view of the nature of paganism evidently
persisted in leading circles.

[1] This was written before the appearance of Mr. Gruppe's work,
Geschichte der klassischen Mythologie und Religionsgeschichte. Compare
infra, p. 154.

We seldom find definite heathen gods so precisely designated as demons as in Milton, but no
doubt seems possible that the general principle
was accepted by contemporary and earlier authors.
The chief work of the seventeenth century on ancient
religion is the *De Theologia Gentili* of G. I. Voss ; he
operates entirely with the traditional view.   It may
be traced back through a succession of writings of
the seventeenth and sixteenth centuries.   They are
all, or almost all, agreed that antique paganism was
the work of the devil, and that idolatry was, at any
rate in part, a worship of demons.   From the
Middle Ages I can adduce a pregnant expression of
the same view from Thomas Aquinas ; in his treatment of idolatry and also of false prophecy he
definitely accepts the demonology of the early
Church.   On this point he appeals to Augustine,
and with perfect right ; from this it may presumably
be assumed that the Schoolmen in general had the
same view, Augustine being, as we know, an authority for Catholic theologians.

In mediaeval poets also we occasionally find the
same view expressed.   As far as I have been able to
ascertain, Dante has no ancient gods among his
devils, and the degree to which he had dissociated
himself from ancient paganism may be gauged by the
fact that in one of the most impassioned passages of
his poem he addresses the Christian God as " Great
Jupiter."   But he allows figures of ancient mythology such as Charon, Minos and Geryon to appear
in his infernal world, and when he designates the
pagan gods as " false and *untruthful*," demonology
is evidently at the back of his mind.   The mediaeval

epic poets who dealt with antique subjects took over the pagan gods more or less.   Sometimes, as in the Romance of Troy, the Christian veneer is so thick that the pagan groundwork is but slightly apparent ; in other poems, such as the adaptation of the *Aeneid*, it is more in evidence.   In so far as the gods are not eliminated they seem as a rule to be taken over quite naïvely from the source without further comment ; but occasionally the poet expresses his view of their nature.   Thus the French adapter of Statius's *Thebaïs*, in whose work the Christian element is otherwise not prominent, cautiously remarks that Jupiter and Tisiphone, by whom his heroes swear, are in reality only devils.   Generally speaking, the gods of antiquity are often designated as devils in mediaeval poetry, but at times the opinion that they are departed human beings crops up.   Thus, as we might expect, the theories of ancient times still survive and retain their sway.

There is a domain in which we might expect to find distinct traces of the survival of the ancient gods in the mediaeval popular consciousness, namely, that of magic.   There does not, however, seem to be much in it ; the forms of mediaeval magic often go back to antiquity, but the beings it operates with are pre-eminently the Christian devils, if we may venture to employ the term, and the evil spirits of popular belief.   There is, however, extant a collection of magic formulae against various ailments in which pagan gods appear : Hercules and Juno Regina, Juno and Jupiter, the nymphs, Luna Jovis filia, Sol invictus.   The collection is transmitted in a manuscript of the ninth century ; the formulae mostly convey the impression of dating from a much earlier period, but the fact that they were copied in the Middle Ages suggests that they were intended for practical application.

A problem, the closer investigation of which would no doubt yield an interesting result, but which does not seem to have been much noticed, is the European conception of the heathen religions with which the explorers came into contact on their great voyages of discovery. Primitive heathenism as a living reality had lain rather beyond the horizon of the Middle Ages ; when it was met with in America, it evidently awakened considerable interest. There is a description of the religion of Peru and Mexico, written by the Jesuit Acosta at the close of the sixteenth century, which gives us a clear insight into the orthodox view of heathenism during the Renaissance. According to Acosta, heathenism is as a whole the work of the Devil ; he has seduced men to idolatry in order that he himself may be worshipped instead of the true God. All worship of idols is in reality worship of Satan. The individual idols, however, are not identified with individual devils ; Acosta distinguishes between the worship of nature (heavenly bodies, natural objects of the earth, right down to trees, etc.), the worship of the dead, and the worship of images, but says nothing about the worship of demons. At one point only is there a direct intervention of the evil powers, namely, in magic, and particularly in oracles ; and here then we find, as an exception, mention of individual devils which must be imagined to inhabit the idols. The same con-

ception is found again as late as the seventeenth
century in a story told by G. I. Voss of the
time of the Dutch wars in Brazil. Arcissewski,
a Polish officer serving in the Dutch army,
had witnessed the conjuring of a devil among the
Tapuis. The demon made his appearance all right,
but proved to be a native well known to Arcissewski.
As he, however, made some true prognostications,
Voss, as it seems at variance with Arcissewski,
thinks that there must have been some supernatural powers concerned in the game.

An exceptional place is occupied by the attempt
made during the Renaissance at an actual revival of
ancient paganism and the worship of its gods. It
proceeded from Plethon, the head of the Florentine
Academy, and seems to have spread thence to the
Roman Academy. The whole movement must be
viewed more particularly as an outcome of the
enthusiasm during the Renaissance for the culture
of antiquity and more especially for its philosophy
rather than its religion ; the gods worshipped were
given a new and strongly philosophical interpretation. But it is not improbable that the traditional
theory of the reality of the ancient deities may have
had something to do with it.

Simultaneously with demonology, and while it
was still acknowledged in principle, there flourished
more naturalistic conceptions of paganism, both in
the Middle Ages and during the Renaissance. As
remarked above, the way was already prepared for
them during antiquity. In Thomas Aquinas we find
a lucid explanation of the origin of idolatry with a
reference to the ancient theory. Here we meet

with the familiar elements : the worship of the stars
and the cult of the dead. According to Thomas,
man has a natural disposition towards this error,
but it only comes into play when he is led astray by
demons. In the sixteenth and seventeenth centuries the Devil is mentioned oftener than the
demons (compare Acosta's view of the heathenism
of the American Indians) ; evidently the conception
of the nature of evil had undergone a change in the
direction of monotheism. In this way more scope
was given for the adoption of naturalistic views in
regard to the individual forms in which paganism
manifested itself than when dealing with a multiplicity of demons that answered individually to the
pagan gods, and we meet with systematic attempts
to explain the origin of idolatry by natural means,
though still with the Devil in the background.

One of these systems, which played a prominent
part, especially in the seventeenth century, is the
so-called Hebraism, *i.e.* the attempt to derive the
whole of paganism from Judaism. This fashion,
for which the way had already been prepared by
Jewish and Christian apologists, reaches its climax,
I think, with Abbot Huet, who derived all the gods
of antiquity (and not only Greek and Roman
antiquity) from Moses, and all the goddesses from
his sister ; according to him the knowledge of these
two persons had spread from the Jews to other
peoples, who had woven about them a web of
" fables." Alongside of Hebraism, which is Euhemeristic in principle, allegorical methods of
interpretation were put forward. The chief representative of this tendency in earlier times is Natalis

Comes (Noël du Comte), the author of the first handbook of mythology; he directly set himself the task of allegorising all the myths. The allegories are mostly moral, but also physical; Euhemeristic interpretations are not rejected either, and in several places the author gives all three explanations side by side without choosing between them. In the footsteps of du Comte follows Bacon, in his *De Sapientia Veterum*; to the moral and physical allegories he adds political ones, as when Jove's struggle with Typhoeus is made to symbolise a wise ruler's treatment of a rebellion. While these attempts at interpretation, both the Euhemeristic and the allegorical, are in principle a direct continuation of those of antiquity, another method points plainly in the direction of the fantastic notions of the Middle Ages. As early as the sixteenth century the idea arose of connecting the theology of the ancients with alchemy. The idea seemed obvious because the metals were designated by the names of the planets, which are also the names of the gods. It found acceptance, and in the seventeenth century we have a series of writings in which ancient mythology is explained as the symbolical language of chemical processes.

Within the limits of the supernatural explanation the interest centred more and more in a single point : the oracles. As far back as in Aquinas, " false prophecy " is a main section in the chapter on demons, whose power to foretell the future he expressly acknowledges. In the sixteenth and seventeenth centuries, when the interest in the prediction of the future was so strong, the ancient

accounts of true prognostications were the real prop
of demonology.   Hence demons generally play a
great part in these explanations, even though in
other cases the Devil fills the bill.   Thus Acosta in
his account of the American religions ; thus Voss and
numerous other writers of the seventeenth century ;
and it is hardly a mere accident, one would think,
when Milton specially mentions Dodona and Delphi
as the seats of worship of the Greek demons.
Among a few of the humanists we certainly find an
attempt to apply the natural explanation even
here ; thus Caelius Rhodiginus asserted that a
great part (but not all !) of the oracular system
might be explained as priestly imposture, and his
slightly younger contemporary Caelius Calcagninus,
in his dialogue on oracles, seems to go still further
and to deny the power of predicting the future to
any other being than the true God.   An exceptional
position is occupied by Pomponazzi, who in his little
pamphlet *De Incantationibus* seems to wish to derive all magic, including the oracles, from natural
causes, though ultimately he formally acknowledges
demonology as the authoritative explanation.   But
these advances did not find acceptance ; we find
even Voss combating the view on which they were
founded.   It is characteristic of the power of demonology in this domain that in support of his point of
view he can quote no less a writer than Machiavelli.

The author who opened battle in real earnest
against demonology was a Dutch scholar, one
van Dale, otherwise little known.   In a couple of
treatises written about the close of the seventeenth
century he tried to show that the whole of idolatry

(as well as the oracles in particular) was not dependent on the intervention of supernatural beings, but
was solely due to imposture on the part of the priests.
Van Dale was a Protestant, so he easily got over
the unanimous recognition of demonology by the
Fathers of the Church.   The accounts of demons in
the Old and New Testaments proved more difficult
to deal with ; it is interesting to see how he wriggles
about to get round them—and it illustrates most
instructively the degree to which demonology affords
the only reasonable and natural explanation of
paganism on the basis of early Christian belief.

Van Dale's books are learned works written in
Latin, full of quotations in Latin, Greek, and
Hebrew, and moreover confused and obscure in
exposition, as is often the case with Dutch writings
of that time.   But a clever Frenchman, Fontenelle,
took upon himself the task of rendering his work on
the oracles into French in a popular and attractive
form.   His book called forth an answering pamphlet
from a Jesuit advocating the traditional view ; the
little controversy seems to have made some stir in
France about the year 1700.   At any rate Banier,
who, in the beginning of the eighteenth century,
treated ancient mythology from a Euhemeristic
point of view, gave some consideration to it.   His
own conclusion is—in 1738 !—that demonology
cannot be dispensed with for the explanation of the
oracles.   He gives his grounds for this in a very
sensible criticism of van Dale's priestly fraud
theory, the absurdity of which he exposes with
sound arguments.

Banier is the last author to whom I can point for

the demon-theory applied as an explanation of a phenomenon in ancient religion ; I have not found it in any other mythologist of the eighteenth century, and even in Banier, with the exception of this single point, everything is explained quite naturally according to the best Euhemeristic models. But in the positive understanding of the nature of ancient paganism no very considerable advance had actually been made withal. A characteristic example of this is the trcatment of ancient religion by such an eminent intellect as Giambattista Vico. In his *Scienza Nuova,* which appeared in 1725, as the foundation of his exposition of the religion of antiquity he gives a characterisation of the mode of thought of primitive mankind, which is so pertinent and psychologically so correct that it anticipates the results of more than a hundred years of research. Of any supernatural explanation no trace is found in him, though otherwise he speaks as a good Catholic. But when he proceeds to explain the nature of the ancient ideas of the gods in detail, all that it comes to is a series of allegories, among which the politico-social play a main part. Vico sees the earliest history of mankind in the light of the traditions about Rome ; the Graeco-Roman gods, then, and the myths about them, become to him largely an expression of struggles betwen the " patricians and plebeians " of remote antiquity.

Most of the mythology of the eighteenth century is like this. The Euhemeristic school gradually gave up the hypothesis of the Jewish religion as the origin of paganism ; Banier, the chief representative of the school, still argues at length against Hebraism.

In its place, Phoenicians, Assyrians, Persians and, above all, Egyptians, are brought into play, or, as in the case of the Englishman Bryant, the whole of mythology is explained as reminiscences of the exploits of an aboriginal race, the Cuthites, which never existed. The allegorist school gradually rallied round the idea of the cult of the heavenly bodies as the origin of the pagan religions ; as late as the days of the French Revolution, Dupuis, in a voluminous work, tried to trace the whole of ancient religion and mythology back to astronomy. On the whole the movement diverged more and more from Euhemerism towards the conception of Greek religion as a kind of cult of nature ; when the sudden awakening to a more correct understanding came towards the close of the century, Euhemerism was evidently already an antiquated view. Thus, since the Renaissance, by a slow and very devious process of development, a gradual approach had been made to a more correct view of the nature of ancient religion. After the Devil had more or less taken the place of the demons, the rest of demonology, the moral allegory, Hebraism and Euhemerism were eliminated by successive stages, and nature-symbolism was reached as the final stage.

We know now that even this is not the correct explanation of the nature and origin of the conception of the gods prevailing among the ancients. Recent investigations have shown that the Greek gods, in spite of their apparent simplicity and clarity, are highly complex organisms, the products of a long process of development to which the most diverse factors have contributed. In order to arrive at this result another century of work, with many attempts in the wrong direction, has been required. The idea that the Greek gods were nature-gods really dominated research through almost the whole of the nineteenth century. If it has now been dethroned or reduced to the measure of truth it contains—for undoubtedly a natural object enters as a component into the essence of some Greek deities—this is in the first place due to the intensive study of the religions of primitive peoples, living or obsolete ; and the results of this study were only applied to Greek religion during the last decade of the century. But the starting-point of modern history of religion lies much farther back : its beginnings date from the great revival of historical research which was inaugurated by Rousseau and continued by Herder. Henceforward the unhistorical methods of the age of enlightenment were abolished, and attention directed in real earnest towards the earlier stages of human civilisation.

This, however, carries us a step beyond the point of time at which this sketch should, strictly speaking, stop. For by the beginning of the eighteenth century—but not before—the negative fact which is all important in this connexion had won recognition : namely, that there existed no supernatural beings latent behind the Greek ideas of their gods, and corresponding at any rate in some degree to them ; but that these ideas must be regarded and explained as entirely inventions of the human imagination.

CHAPTER IX

AT the very beginning of this inquiry it was emphasised that its theme would in the main be the religious views of the upper class, and within this sphere again especially the views of those circles which were in close touch with philosophy. The reason for this is of course in the first place that only in such circles can we expect to find expressed a point of view approaching to positive atheism. But we may assuredly go further than this. We shall hardly be too bold in asserting that the free-thinking of philosophically educated men in reality had very slight influence on the great mass of the population. Philosophy did not penetrate so far, and whatever degree of perception we estimate the masses to have had of the fact that the upper layer of society regarded the popular faith with critical eyes—and in the long run it could not be concealed — we cannot fail to recognise that religious development among the ancients did not tend towards atheism. Important changes took place in ancient religion during the Hellenistic Age and the time of the Roman Empire, but their causes were of a social and national kind, and, if we confine ourselves to paganism, they only led to certain gods going out of fashion and others coming in. The utmost we can assert is that a certain weakening

of the religious life may have been widely prevalent
during the time of transition between the two ages—
the transition falls at somewhat different dates in
the eastern and western part of the Empire—but
that weakening was soon overcome.

Now the peculiar result of this investigation of
the state of religion among the upper classes seems
to me to be this : the curve of intensity of religious
feeling which conjecture leads us to draw through
the spiritual life of the ancients as a whole, that
same curve, but more distinct and sharply accen-
tuated, is found again in the relations of the upper
classes to the popular faith.   Towards the close of
the fifth century it looks as if the cultured classes
that formed the centre of Greek intellectual life were
outgrowing   the   ancient   religion.   The   reaction
which set in with Socrates and Plato certainly
checked this movement, but it did not stop it.
Cynics,   Peripatetics,   Stoics,   Epicureans   and
Sceptics, in spite of their widely differing points of
view, were all entirely unable to share the religious
ideas of their countrymen in the form in which they
were cast in the national religion.   However many
allowances they made, their attitude towards the
popular faith was critical, and on important points
they denied it.   It is against the background thus
resulting from ancient philosophy's treatment of
ancient religion that we must view such phenomena
as Polybius, Cicero, and Pliny the Elder, if we wish
to understand their full significance.

On the other hand, it is certain that this was not
the view that conquered in the end among the
educated classes in antiquity.   The lower we come

down in the Empire the more evident does the positive relation of the upper class to the gods of the
popular faith become. Some few examples have
already been mentioned in the preceding pages. In
philosophy the whole movement finds its typical
expression in demonology, which during the later
Empire reigned undisputed in the one or two schools
that still retained any vitality. It is significant
that its source was the earlier Platonism, with its
very conservative attitude towards popular belief,
and that it was taken over by the later Stoic school,
which inaugurated the general religious reaction
in philosophy. And it is no less significant that
demonology was swallowed whole by the monotheistic religion which superseded ancient paganism,
and for more than a thousand years was the recognised explanation of the nature thereof.

In accordance with the line of development here
sketched, the inquiry has of necessity been focused
on two main points : Sophistic and the Hellenistic
Age. Now it is of peculiar interest to note what small
traces of pure atheism can after all be found here,
in spite of all criticism of the popular faith. We
have surmised its presence among a few prominent
personalities in fifth - century Athens ; we have
found evidence of its extension in the same place
in the period immediately following ; and in the
time of transition between the fourth and third
centuries we have thought it likely that it existed
among a very few philosophers, of whom none are in
the first rank. Everywhere else we find adjustments,
in part very serious and real concessions, to popular
belief. Not to mention the attitude towards wor-

ship, which was only hostile in one sect of slight importance : the assumption of the divinity of the heavenly bodies which was common to the Academics, Peripatetics, and Stoics is really in principle an acknowledgement of the popular faith, whose conception of the gods was actually borrowed and applied, not to some philosophical abstraction, but to individual and concrete natural objects. The anthropomorphic gods of the Epicureans point in the same direction. In spite of their profound difference from the beings that were worshipped and believed in by the ordinary Greek, they are in complete harmony with the opinion on which all polytheism is based : that there are individual beings of a higher order than man. And though the Stoics in theory confined their acknowledgment of this doctrine to the heavenly bodies, in practice— even if we disregard demonology—they consistently brought it to bear upon the anthropomorphic gods, in direct continuation of the Socratic reaction against the atheistic tendencies of Sophistic.

If now we ask ourselves what may be the cause of this peculiar dualism in the relationship of ancient thought to religion, though admitting the highly complex nature of the problem, we can scarcely avoid recognising a certain principle. Ancient thought outgrew the ancient popular faith ; that is beyond doubt. Hence its critical attitude. But it never outgrew that supernaturalist view which was the foundation of the popular faith. Hence its concessions to the popular faith, even when it was most critical, and its final surrender thereunto. And that it never outgrew the founda-

11

tion of the popular faith is connected with its whole
conception of nature and especially with its conception of the universe. We cannot indeed deny
that the ancients had a certain feeling that nature
was regulated by laws, but they only made imperfect
attempts at a mechanical theory of nature in which
this regulation of the world by law was carried
through in principle, and with one brilliant exception
they adhered implicitly to the geocentric conception of the universe. We may, I think, venture to
assert with good reason that on such assumptions
the philosophers of antiquity could not advance
further than they did. In other words, on the given
hypotheses the supernaturalist view was the correct
one, the one that was most probable, and therefore
that on which people finally agreed. A few chosen
spirits may at any time by intuition, without any
strictly scientific foundation, emancipate themselves entirely from religious errors ; this also happened among the ancients, and on the first occasion
was not unconnected with an enormous advance in
the conception of nature. But it is certain that the
views of an entire age are always decisively conditioned by its knowledge and interpretation of the
universe surrounding it, and cannot in principle be
emancipated therefrom.

Seen from this point of view, our brief sketch of
the attitude of posterity towards the religion of the
pagan world will also not be without interest. If,
after isolated advances during the mighty awakening of the Renaissance, it is not until the transition
from the seventeenth to the eighteenth century that
we find the modern atheistic conception of the

nature of the gods of the ancients established in
principle and consistently applied, we can scarcely
avoid connecting this fact with the advance of
natural science in the seventeenth century, and not
least with the victory of the heliocentric system.
After the close of antiquity the pagan gods had re-
ceded to a distance, practically speaking, because
they were not worshipped any more. No one
troubled himself about them. But in theory one
had got no further, *i.e.* no advance had been made
on the ancients, and no advance could be made
as long as supernaturalism was adhered to in
connexion with the ancient view of the universe.
Through monotheism the notions of the divinity
of the sun, moon and planets had certainly been got
rid of, but not so the notion of the world—*i.e.* the
globe enclosed within the firmament—as filled with
personal beings of a higher order than man ; and
even the duty of turning the spheres to which the
heavenly bodies were believed to be fastened was—
quite consistently—assigned to some of these beings.
As long as such notions were in operation, not only
were there no grounds for denying the reality of the
pagan gods, but there was every reason to assume it.
So far we may rightly say that it was Copernicus,
Galileo, Giordano Bruno, Kepler and Newton that
did away with the traditional conception of ancient
paganism.

Natural science, however, furnishes only the
negative result that the gods of polytheism are not
what they are said to be : real beings of a higher
order than man. To reveal what they are, other
knowledge is required. This was not attained until

long after the revival of natural science in the sixteenth and seventeenth centuries.   The vacillation
in the eighteenth century between various theories
of the explanation of the nature of ancient polytheism
—theories which were all false, though not equally
false—is in this respect significant enough ; likewise
the gradual progress which characterises research
in the nineteenth century, and which may be indicated by such names as Heyne, Buttmann, K. O.
Müller, Lobeck, Mannhardt, Rohde, and Usener,
to mention only some of the most important and
omitting those still alive.   Viewed in this light
the development sketched here within a narrowly
restricted field is typical of the course of European
intellectual history from antiquity down to our day.

NOTES

OF Atheism in Antiquity as defined here no treatment is known
to me ; but there exist an older and a newer book that deal with
the question within a wider compass.   The first of these is Krische,
Die theologischen Lehren der griechischen Denker (Göttingen, 1840);
it is chiefly concerned with the philosophical conceptions of deity,
but it touches also on the relations of philosophers to popular
religion.   The second is Decharme, *La critique des traditions
religieuses chez les Grecs* (Paris, 1904); it is not fertile in new points
of view, but it has suggested several details which I might else
have overlooked.   Such books as Caird, *The Evolution of Theology
in the Greek Philosophers* (Glasgow, 1904), or Moon, *Religious
Thought of the Greeks* (Cambridge, Mass., 1919), barely touch on
the relation to popular belief ; of Louis, *Les doctrines religieuses
des philosophes grecs,* I have not been able to make use.   I regret
that Poul Helms, *The Conception of God in Greek Philosophy*
(Danish, in *Studier for Sprog- og Oldtidsforskning,* No. 115), was not
published until my essay was already in the press.   General works
on Atheism are indicated in Aveling's article, "Atheism," in the
Catholic Encyclopædia, vol. ii., but none of them seem to be found
at Copenhagen.   In the *Dictionary of Religion and Ethics,* ii.,
there is a detailed article on Atheism in its relation to different
religions ; the section treating of Antiquity is written by Pearson,
but is meagre.   Works like Zeller, *Philosophie der Griechen,* and
Gomperz, *Griechische Denker,* contain accounts of the attitude of
philosophers (Gomperz also includes others) towards popular
belief ; of these books I have of course made use throughout, but
they are not referred to in the following notes except on special
occasion.   Scattered remarks and small monographs on details
are naturally to be found in plenty.   Where I have met with
such and found something useful in them, or where I express
dissent from them, I have noticed it ; but I have not aimed at
exhausting the literature on my subject.   On the other hand I
have tried to make myself completely acquainted with the first-
hand material, wherever it gave a direct support for assuming
Atheism, and to take my own view of it.   In many cases, however,
the argumentation has had to be indirect : it has been necessary
to draw inferences from what an author does not say in a certain
connexion when he might be expected to say it, or what he generally and throughout avoids mentioning, or from his general
manner and peculiarities in his way of speaking of the gods.   In
such cases I have often had to be content with my previous knowledge and my general impression of the facts ; but then I have

as a rule made use of the important modern literature on the subject. In working out the sketch of the ideas after the end of Antiquity, I have been almost without any guidance in modern literature. I have accordingly had to try, on the basis of a superficial acquaintance with some of the chief types, to form for myself, as best I might, some idea of the course of the evolution ; but I have not been able to go systematically through the immense material, however fruitful such a research appeared to be. In the meantime, between the publication of my Danish essay and this translation, there has appeared a work by Mr. Gruppe, *Geschichte der klassischen Mythologie und Religionsgeschichte* (Leipzig, 1921). My task in writing my last chapters would have been much easier if I could have made use of Mr. Gruppe's learned and comprehensive treatment of the subject ; but it would not have been superfluous, for Mr. Gruppe deals principally with the history of classical mythology, not with the history of the belief in the gods of antiquity. So I have ventured to let my sketch stand as it is, only reducing some of the notes (which I had on purpose made rather full, to aid others who might pursue the subject) by referring to Mr. Gruppe instead of to the sources themselves.

For kindly helping me to find my bearings in out-of-the-way parts of my subject, I am indebted to my colleagues F. Buhl, I. L. Heiberg, I. C. Jacobsen and Kr. Nyrop, as well as to Prof. Martin P. Nilsson in Lund.

P. 1. Definition of Atheism : see the article in the *Catholic Encycl.* vol. ii.

P. 5. Atheism : see Murray, *New Engl. Dict.*, under Atheism and -ism. The word seems to have come up in the Renaissance.

P. 6. Criminal Law at Athens : see Lipsius, *Das attische Recht und Rechtsverfahren*, i. p. 358.—The definition in Aristotle, *de virt. et vit.* 7, p. 1251a, has, I think, no legal foundation.

P. 9. On the legal foundation for the trials of Christians, see Mommsen, *Der Religionsfrevel nach römischem Recht* (*Ges. Schr.* iii. p. 389).—Mommsen goes too far, I think, in supposing a legal foundation for the trials of Christians ; above all, I do not believe that the defection from the Roman religion was ever considered as *maiestas* in the technical sense of the word, the more so as it is certain that, after the earliest period, no difference was made in the treatment of citizens and aliens.

P. 13. Lists of atheists : Cicero, *de nat. deor.* 1. 1, 2 (comp. 1. 23, 26). Sext. Emp. *hypotyp.* 3. 213 ; *adv. math.* 9. 50. Aelian, *v.h.* 2. 31 ; *de nat. an.* 6. 40.—The predicate *atheos* is once applied to Anaxagoras by a Christian author (Irenaeus : see Diels, *Vorsokr.* 46, A 113 ; compare also Marcellinus, *vit. Thuc.* (see below, note on p. 29). Of such isolated cases I have taken no account.

P. 16. On the dualism in the Greek conception of the nature of gods see Nägelsbach, *Hom. Theol.* p. 11.—Pindar : *Ol.* 1. 28, 9. 35 ; *Pyth.* 3. 27.

P. 17. Xenophanes : Einhorn, *Zeit- und Streitfragen der modernen Xenophanesforschung* (*Arch. f. Gesch. d. Philos.* xxxi.).

P. 18. Xenophanes's age : Diels, *Vorsokr.* 11, B 8.—His criticism of Homer and Hesiod : *ibid.* 11, 12.—Titans and Giants :

ibid. 1. 22.—Criticism of Anthropomorphism : *ibid.* 14–16.—
Divination : Cic. *de div.* 1. 3, 5.

P. 19. On Xenophanes's conception of God, comp. *Vorsokr.*
11, B 23–26 ; on the identification of God with the universe:
Vorsokr. 11, A 30, 31, 33–36.—Cicero : *de div.* 1. 3, 5.

P. 21. For Xenophanes's theology, comp. Freudenthal, *Arch.
f. Gesch. d. Philos.* i. p. 322, and Zeller's criticism, *ibid.* p. 524.
Agreeing with Freudenthal : Decharme, p. 46 ; Campbell, *Religion
in Greek Literature,* p. 293.

P. 21. Parmenides does not even appear to have designated
his " Being " as God (Zeller, i. p. 563).

P. 23. In the eighteenth century people discussed diffusely
the question whether Thales was an atheist (of course in the
sense in which the word was taken at that time) ; comp. Tennemann, *Gesch. d. Philos.* i. pp. 62 and 422. Tennemann remarks
quite truly that the question is put wrongly.

P. 24. Thales : Diels, *Vorsokr.* 1, A 22–23.—Attitude of
Democritus towards popular belief : *Vorsokr.* 55, A 74–79 ; comp.
116, 117 ; B 166, and also B 30. Diels, *Ueber den Dämonenglauben
des D.* (*Arch. f. Gesch. d. Philos.* 1894, p. 154).

P. 25. Trial of Anaxagoras : *Vorsokr.* 46, A 1, 17, 18, 19.

P. 26. Ram's head : *Vorsokr.* 46, A 16.

P. 27. Geffcken (in *Hermes,* 42, p. 127) has tried to make out
something about a criticism of popular belief by Anaxagoras
from some passages in Aristophanes (*Nub.* 398) and Lucian (*Tim.*
10, etc.), but I do not think he has succeeded. Pericles a free-
thinker : Plut. *Pericl.* 6 and 38 ; comp. Decharme, p. 160.—
Personality of Anaxagoras : *Vorsokr.* 46, A 30 (Aristotle, *Eud.
Ethics,* A 4, p. 1215*b,* 6).

P. 28. Herodotus : 8, 77.—Sophocles : *Oed. rex.* 498, 863.—
Diopeithes : Plut. *Pericl.* 32 (*Vorsokr.* 46, A 17).—Thucydides :
Classen in the preface to his 3rd ed., p. lvii.

P. 29. Thucydides, a disciple of Anaxagoras : Marcellinus,
vit. Thuc. 22.—Generally Thucydides is thought to have been more
conservative in his religious opinions than I consider probable ;
see Classen, *loc. cit.* ; Decharme, p. 83 ; Gertz in his preface to the
Danish translation of Thucydides, p. xxvii.—Hippo : *Vorsokr.* 26,
A 4, 6, 8, 9 ; B 2, 3.

P. 30. Aristotle : *Vorsokr.* 26, A 7.—Diogenes an atheist:
Aelian, *v.h.* 2, 31.—The air his god : *Vorsokr.* 51, A 8 (he thought
that Homer identified Zeus with the air, and approved of this as
οὐ μυθικῶς, ἀλλ᾽ ἀληθῶς εἰρημένον) ; B 5. 7, 8.—Allusions to his doctrines
by Aristophanes : *Nub.* 225, 828 (*Vorsokr.* 51, C 1, 2).

P. 31. A chief representative of the naïvely critical view of
natural phenomena is for us Herodotus. The *locus classicus* is
vii. 129 ; comp. Gomperz, *Griech. Denker,* i. p. 208 ; Heiberg,
Festskrift til Ussing (Copenhagen, 1900), p. 91 ; Decharme, p. 69.—
Principal passages about Diagoras : Sext. Emp. *adv. math.* 9, 53 ;
Suidas, art. *Diagoras II.*) ; schol. Aristoph. *Nub.* 830 (the legend);
Suidas, art. *Diagoras I.*) ; Aristoph. *Av.* 1071 with schol.; schol.
Aristoph. *Ran.* 320 ; [Lysias] vi. 17 ; Diod. xiii. 16 (the decree) ;
Philodem. *de piet.* p. 89 Gomp. (comments of Aristoxenus) ;

Aelian, *v.h.* ii. 22 (legislation at Mantinea).—Wilamowitz (*Textgesch. d. Lyr.* p. 80) has tried to save the tradition by supposing that the *acme* of Diagoras has been put too early. Comp. also his remarks, *Griech. Verskunst.* p. 426, where he has taken up the question again with reference to my treatment of it. As he has now conceded the possibility of referring the legislation to the earlier date, the difference between us is really very slight, and it is of course possible, perhaps even probable, that the acme of the poet has been antedated.—Aristoph. *Av.* 1071 : "On this very day it is made public, that if one of you kills Diagoras from Melos, he shall have a talent, and if one kills one of the dead tyrants, he shall have a talent." The parallel between the two decrees, of which the latter is of course an invention of Aristophanes, would be without point if the decree against Diagoras was not as futile as the decree against the tyrants (*i.e.* the sons of Peisistratus, who had been dead some three-quarters of a century), that is, if it did not come many years too late.—Wilamowitz (*Griech. Verskunst, loc. cit.*) takes the sense to be : " You will not get hold of Diagoras any more than you did of the tyrants." But this, besides being somewhat pointless, does not agree so well as my explanation with the introductory words : "On this very day." On the other hand, I never meant to imply that Diagoras was dead in 415, but only that his offence was an old one—just as that of Protagoras probably was (see p. 39).

P. 39. Trial of Protagoras : *Vorsokr.* 74, A 1–4, 23 ; the passage referring to the gods : *ibid.* B 4.—Plato : *Theaet.* p. 162d (*Vorsokr.* 74, A 23).

P. 41. Distinction between belief and knowledge by Protagoras : Gomperz, *Griech. Denker,* i. p. 359.

P. 42. Prodicus : *Vorsokr.* 77, B 5. Comp. Norvin, *Allegorien i den græske Philosophi* (*Edda,* 1919), p. 82. I cannot, however, quite adopt Norvin's view of the theory of Protagoras.

P. 44. Critias : *Vorsokr.* 81, B 25.—W. Nestle, *Jahrbb. f. Philol.* xi. (1903), pp. 81 and 178, gives an exhaustive treatment of the subject, but I cannot share his view of it.

P. 46. Euripides : *Suppl.* 201.—Moschion : *Trag. Fragm.* ed. Nauck (2nd ed.), p. 813.—Plato : *Rep.* ii. 369b.

P. 47. Democritus : Reinhardt in *Hermes,* xlvii (1912), p. 503 In spite of Wilamowitz's objections (in his *Platon,* ii. p. 214), I still consider it probable that Plato alludes to a philosophical theory.— Protagoras on the original state : *Vorsokr.* 74, B 8b.

P. 48. Euripides : *Electra,* 737 (Euripides does not believe in the tale that the sun reversed its course on account of Thyestes's fraud against Atreus, and then adds : " Fables that terrify men are a profit to the worship of the gods ").—Aristotle : *Metaph.* Λ 8, 1074b ; see text, p. 85.—Polybius : vi. 56 ; see text pp. 90 and 114.—Plato's *Gorgias,* p. 482 and foll.

P. 49.—Callicles : see *e.g.* Wilamowitz, *Platon,* i. p. 208.

P. 50.—Thrasymachus : Plato, *Rep.* i. pp. 338c, 343a ; comp. also ii. p. 358b. His remark on Providence (*Vorsokr.* 78, B 8) runs thus : " The gods do not see the things that are done among men ; if they did, they would not overlook the greatest human good,

justice. For we find that men do not follow it." Comp. text,
p. 61.—Diagoras as Critias's source : Nestle, *Jahrbb.*, 1903, p. 101.

P. 51. Euripides : see W. Nestle, *Euripides* (Stuttgart, 1901)
pp. 51–152. Here, too, the material is set forth exhaustively ; the
results seem to me inadmissible. Browning's theory (*The Ring
and the Book*, x. 1661 foll.) that Euripides did believe in the existence of the gods, but did not believe them to be perfect, is a possible,
perhaps even a probable, explanation of many of his utterances ;
but it will hardly fit all of them. I have examined the question
in an essay, "Browning om Euripides " in my *Udvalgte Afhandlinger*, p. 55.

P. 52. Gods identified with the Elements : *Bacch.* 274 ; fragm.
839, 877, 941 (Nestle, p. 153).

P. 53. Polemic against sophists : Nestle, p. 206.—*Bellerophon :*
fragm. 286.

P. 54. " If the gods——" : fragm. 292, 7.

P. 55. *Melanippe* : fragm. 480. The words are said to have
given offence at the rehearsal, so that Euripides altered them at
the production of the play (Plut. *Amat.* ch. 13).—Aeschylus :
Agam. 160.—Aristophanes : *Thesmoph.* 450.—In the *Frogs*, 892,
Euripides prays to the Ether and other abstractions, not to the
gods.—*Clouds* : 1371.

P. 56. Plato : *Republ.* viii. p. 568*a*.—Quotation from *Melanippe :* Plut. *Amat.* 13.

P. 57. Aristophanes and Naturalism : see note to p. 30.

P. 58. Denial of the gods in the *Clouds*, 247, 367, 380, 423, 627,
817, 825, 1232.—Moral of the piece : 1452–1510.—In Aristophanes's
own travesties of the gods, scholars have found evidence for a
weakening of popular belief, but this is certainly wrong ; comp.
Decharme, p. 109.—Words like " believe " and " belief " do not
cover the Greek word νομίζειν, which signifies at once "believe "
and " be in the habit," " use habitually," so that it covers both
belief and worship—an ambiguity that is characteristic of Greek
religion.—Xenophon : *Memorab.* i. 1 ; *Apol. Socr.* 10 and foll.

P. 59. Plato : *Apol.* p. 24*b* (the indictment) ; 26*b* (the re-
futation).

P. 60. Aristodemus : Xenoph. *Memor.* i. 4.—Cinesias : Decharme, p. 135.—The Hermocopidae : Decharme, p. 152. Beloch,
Hist. of Greece, ii. 1, p. 360, has another explanation. To my argument it is of no consequence what special motive is assigned for
the crime, as long as it is a political one.

P. 61. Plato on impiety : *Laws*, x. p. 886*b* ; comp. xii. p. 967*a*.
Curiously enough, the same tripartition of the wrong attitude
towards the gods occurs already in the *Republic*, ii. p. 365*d*,
where it is introduced incidentally as well known and a matter
of course.

P. 62. Euripides : *e.g. Hecuba*, 488 ; *Suppl.* 608.—Reference
to Anaxagoras : *Laws*, x. p. 886*d* ; to Sophistic, 889*b*.

P. 65. Plato in the *Apology* : p. 19*c*.—Socrates's *daimonion*
a proof of *asebeia* : Xenoph. *Memorab.* i. 1, 2 ; *Apol. Socr.* 12 ;
Plato, *Apol.* p. 31*d*.

P. 66. Accusation of teaching the doctrine of Anaxagoras :

Plato, *Apol.* p. 26*d* ; comp. Xenoph. *Memor.* i. 1, 10.—Plato's defence of Socrates : *Apol.* p. 27*a.*

P. 67. Xenophon's defence of Socrates : *Memor.* i. 1, 2 ; 6 foll., 10 foll.—Teleological view of nature : Xenoph. *Memor.* i. 4 ; iv. 3.— On the religious standpoint of Socrates, comp. my *Udvalgte Afhandlinger,* p. 38.

P. 68. Plato's *Apology,* p. 21*d,* 23*a* and *f,* etc.—The gods all-knowing : *Odyss.* iv. 379 and 468 ; comp. Nägelsbach, *Hom. Theol.* p. 18 ; *Nachhom. Theol.* p. 23.

P. 69. The gods just : Nägelsbach, *Hom. Theol.* p. 297 ; *Nachhom. Theol.* p. 27.

P. 71. The relation between early religious thought and Delphi has been explained correctly by Sam Wide, *Einleit. in die Altertumswissensch.,* ii. p. 221 ; comp. also I. L. Heiberg in *Tilskueren,* 1919, ii. p. 44.—Honours shown to Pindar at Delphi : schol. Pind. ed. Drachm. i. p. 2, 14 ; 5, 6. Pausan. x. 24. 5.

P. 72. Plato on the Delphic Oracle : *Apol.* p. 20*e.* On the following comp. I. L. Heiberg, *loc. cit.* p. 45.—Socrates on his *daimonion* : Plato, *Apol.* p. 31*c.*

P. 74. Antisthenes : Ritter, *Hist. philos. Gr.*[9] 285.—On the later Cynics, especially Diogenes, see Diog. Laert. vi. 105 (the gods are in need of nothing) ; Julian, *Or.* vi. p. 199*b* (Diogenes did not worship the gods).

P. 75. Cyrenaics : Diog. Laert. ii. 91.—Date of Theodorus : Diog. Laert. ii. 101, 103 ; his book on the gods : Diog. Laert. ii. 97, Sext. Emp. *adv. math.* ix. 55 ; his trial : Diog. Laert. ii. 101.

P. 76. Theodorus's book used by Epicurus : Diog. Laert. ii. 97. —Zeller : *Philos. d. Griechen,* ii. 1, p. 925.—Euthyphron : see especially p. 14*b* foll.

P. 77. Criticism of Mythology in the *Republic* : ii. p. 377*b* foll. ; worship presupposed : *e.g.* iii. p. 415*e* ; v. p. 459*e,* 461*a,* 468*d,* 469*a,* 470*a* ; vii. p. 540*b* ; reference to the Oracle : iv. p. 427*b.*—*Timaeus* : p. 40*d* foll.—*Laws,* rules of worship : vi. p. 759*a,* vii. p. 967*a* and elsewhere, x. p. 909*d* ; capital punishment for atheists : x. p. 909*a.* Comp. above, on p. 61.

P. 78. Atheism a sin of youth : *Laws,* x. p. 888*a.*—Goodness and truth of the gods : *Republ.* ii. p. 379*a,* 380*d,* 382*a.*—Belief in Providence : *Laws,* x. p. 885*c,* etc. ; *Republ.* x. p. 612*e* ; *Apol.* p. 41*d.*

P. 79. *Laws,* x. p. 888*d,* 893*b* foll., especially 899*c–d* ; comp. also xii. p. 967*a–c.*—*Timaeus* : p. 40*d–f.* Comp. *Laws,* xii. p. 948*b.*

P. 80. The gods in the *Republic,* ii. p. 380*d.* This passage, taken together with Plato's general treatment of popular belief, might lead to the hypothesis that it was Plato's doctrine of ideas rather than the rationalism of his youth that brought about strained relations between his thought and popular belief. I incline to think that such is the case ; but there is a long step even from such a state of things to downright atheism, and the stress Plato always laid on the belief in Providence is a strong argument in favour of his belief in the gods, for he could never make his ideas act in the capacity of Providence.—The gods as creators of mankind : *Timaeus,* p. 41*a* foll.

P. 81. Xenocrates : the exposition of his doctrine given in the text is based upon Heinze's *Xenokrates* (Leipzig, 1892).

P. 83. Trial of Aristotle : Diog. Laert. v. 5 ; Athen. xv. p. 696.— The writings of Aristotle that have come down to us are almost all of them compositions for the use of his disciples, and were not accessible to the general public during his lifetime.

P. 84. On the religious views of Aristotle see in general Zeller, ii. 2, p. 787 (Engl. transl. ii. p. 325) ; where the references to his writings are given in full. In the following I indicate only a few passages of special interest.—Discussion of worship precluded : *Top.* A, xi. p. 105*a*, 5.—Aristotle's Will : Diog. Laert. v. 15.—The gods as determining the limits of the human : *e.g. Nic. Eth.* K, viii. p. 1178*b*, 33 : "(the wise) will also be in need of outward prosperity, as he is (only) a man."—Reservations in speaking of the gods, *e.g. Nic. Eth.* K, ix. p. 1179*a*, 13 : "he who is active in accordance with reason . . . must also be supposed to be the most beloved of the gods ; for if the gods trouble themselves about human affairs—*and that they do so is generally taken for granted*—it must be probable that they take pleasure in what is best and most nearly related to themselves (*and that must be the reason*), and that they reward those who love and honour this most highly," etc. The passage is typical both of the hypothetical way of speaking, and of the twist in the direction of Aristotle's own conception of the deity (whose essence is reason) ; also of the Socratic manner of dealing with the gods.

P. 85. The passage quoted is from the *Metaphysics*, Λ viii. p. 1074*a*, 38. Comp. *Metaph.* B, ii. p. 997*b*, 8 ; iv. p. 1000*a*, 9.

P. 86. Theophrastus : Diog. Laert. v. 37.

P. 87. Strato : Diels, *Ueber das physikal. System des S., Sitzungsber. d. Berl. Akad.*, 1893, p. 101.—His god the same as nature : Cic. *de nat. deor.* i. 35.

P. 89. On the history of Hellenistic religion, see Wendland, *Die hellenistisch-römische Kultur in ihren Beziehungen z. Judentum u. Christentum* (Tübingen, 1907).

P. 90. The passage quoted is Polyb. vi. 56, 6.

P. 92. On the Tyche-Religion, see Nägelsbach, *Nachhom. Theologie*, p. 153 ; Lehrs, *Populäre Aufsätze*, p. 153 ; Rohde, *Griech. Roman*, p. 267 (1st ed.) ; Wendland, p. 59.—Thucydides : see Classen in the introduction to his (3rd) edition, pp. lvii–lix, where all the material is collected. A conclusive passage is vii. 36, 6, where Thuc. makes the bigoted Nicias before a decisive battle express the hope that "Fortune" will favour the Athenians.— Demosthenes's dream : *Aeschin.* iii. 77.—Demosthenes on Tyche : *Olynth.* ii. 22 ; *de cor.* 252.

P. 93. Demosthenes and the Pythia : *Aesch.* iii. 130. Comp. *ibid.* 68, 131, 152 ; Plutarch, *Dem.* 20.—Demetrius of Phalerum : Polyb. xxix. 21.—Temples of Tyche : Roscher, *Mythol. Lex.*, art. *Fortuna*.

P. 94. Tyche mistress of the gods : *Trag. adesp. fragm.* 506, Nauck ; [Dio Chrys.] lxiv. p. 331 R.—Polybius : i. 1 ; iii. 5, 7.— The reservations against Tyche as a principle for the explaining of historical facts, and the twisting of the notion in the direction of

Providence found in certain passages in Polybius, do not concern us here ; they are probably due to the Stoic influence he underwent during his stay at Rome. Comp. below, on p. 114, and see Cuntz, *Polybios* (Leipzig, 1902), p. 43.—Pliny : ii. 22 foll.

P. 95. Tyche in the novels : Rohde, *Griech. Rom.* p. 280.

P. 97. Strabo : xvii. p. 813.—Plutarch : *de def. or.* 5 and 7.

P. 98. The Aetolians at Dium : Polyb. iv. 62 ; at Dodona, iv. 67 ; Philip at Thermon, v. 9 ; Dicaearchus, xviii. 54.—Decay of Roman worship : Wissowa, *Religion u. Kultus d. Römer*, p. 70 (2nd ed.). To this work I must refer for indications of the sources ; but the polemic in the text is chiefly directed against Wissowa.

P. 99. Ennius : comp. below, p. 112.

P. 100. Varro : in Augustine, *de civ. Dei*, vi. 2.

P. 103. Theology of the Stoics : Zeller, iii. 1, p. 309–45.

P. 104. Demonology of the Stoics : Heinze, *Xenokrates*, p. 96.

P. 105. Epicurus's theology : Zeller, iii. 1, pp. 427–38. Comp. Schwartz, *Charakterköpfe*, ii. p. 43.

P. 106. Epicurus's doctrine of the eternity of the gods criticised : Cic. *de nat. deor.* i. 68 foll.

P. 107. The Sceptics : Zeller, iii. 1, pp. 507 and 521.

P. 109. Diogenes : see note on p. 74.—Bion : Diog. Laert. iv. 52 and 54.

P. 110. Menippos : R. Helm, *Lukian u. Menipp* (Leipzig and Berlin, 1906).

P. 111. Euhemerus : Jacoby in Pauly-Wissowa's *Realencyclop.*, art. "Euemeros" ; Wendland, *Hellenist. Kultur*, p. 70.—Euhemerism before Euhemerus : Lobeck, *Aglaophamus*, p. 9 ; Wendland, p. 67.

P. 112. A Danish scholar, Dr. J. P. Jacobsen (*Afhandlinger og Artikler*, p. 490), seems to think that Euhemerus's theory was influenced by the worship of heroes. But there is nothing to show that Euhemerus supposed his gods to have continued their existence after their death, though this would have been in accordance with Greek belief even in the Hellenistic period ; he seems rather to have insisted that they were worshipped as gods during their lifetime (comp. Jacoby, *loc. cit.*).

P. 114. Euhemerism in Polybius : xxxiv. 2 ; comp. x. 10, 11.—Relapse into orthodoxy : xxxvii. 9 (the decisive passage) ; xxxix. 19, 2 (concluding prayer to the gods) ; xviii. 54, 7–10 ; xxiii. 10, 14 (the gods punish impiety ; comp. xxxvii. 9, 16). There is a marked contrast between such passages and the way Polybius speaks of Philip's destruction of the sanctuary at Thermon ; he blames it severely, but merely on political, not on religious grounds (v. 9–12). Orthodox utterances in the older portions of the work (i. 84, 10 ; x. 2, 7) may be due to that accommodation to popular belief which Polybius himself acknowledges as justifiable (xvi. 12, 9), but also to later revision.—Influence of Stoicism : Hirzel, *Untersuchungen zu Ciceros philos. Schriften*, ii. p. 841.

P. 115. Cicero's Stoicism in his philosophy of religion : *de nat. deor.* iii. 40, 95.

P. 116. Sanctuary to Tullia : Cic. *ad Att.* xii. 18 foll. ; several of the letters (23, 25, 35, 36) show that Atticus disapproved of the idea, and that Cicero himself was conscious that it was unworthy of him.

P. 117. Euhemeristic defence : *fragm. consol.* 14, 15.—Augustus's reorganisation of the cults : Wissowa, *Religion u. Kultus d. Römer*, p. 73. Recent scholars, especially when treating of Virgil (Heinze, *Vergils ep. Technik*, 3rd ed. p. 291 ; Norden, *Aeneis*, vi. 2nd ed. pp. 314, 318, 362), speak of the reform of Augustus as if it involved a real revulsion of feeling in his contemporaries. This is in my opinion a complete misunderstanding of the facts. Virgil's religious views : *Catal.* v., *Georgics*, ii. 458.

P. 118. Pliny : *hist. nat.* ii. 1–27. The passages translated are §§ 14 and 27.

P. 122. Seneca : fragm. 31–39, Haase.—Stoic polemic against atheism : Epictetus, *diss.* ii. 20, 21 ; comp. Marcus Aurelius, vi. 44.—Later Cynicism : Zeller, iii. 1, p. 763.—Oenomaus : only preserved in excerpts by Euseb. *praep. evang.* 5–6 (a separate edition is wanted).—His polemic directed against the priests : Euseb. 5, p. 213*c* ; comp. Oenomaus himself, *ibid.* 6, p. 256*d*.

P. 123. Lucian : see Christ, *Gesch. d. griech. Litt.* ii. 2, p. 550 (5th ed.), and R. Helm, *Lukian u. Menipp* (see note to p. 110).

P. 124. Timon : ch. x.

P. 126. On Lucian's caution in attacking the really popular gods, see Wilamowitz, in *Kultur d. Gegenwart*, i. 8, p. 248.—The Jews atheists : Harnack, *Der Vorwurf d. Atheismus in den 3 ersten Jahrh.* (*Texte u. Unters.*, N.F., xiii. 4), p. 3.

P. 127. I have met with no comprehensive treatment of Jewish and Christian polemic against Paganism ; Geffcken, *Zwei griech. Apologeten* (Leipzig, 1907), is chiefly concerned with investigations into the sources. I shall therefore indicate the principal passages on which my treatment is based.—Polemic against images in the Old Testament : Isaiah 44. 10 etc. ; in later literature : Epistle of Jeremiah ; Wisdom of Solomon 13 foll. ; Philo, *de decal.* 65 foll., etc.—Euhemerism : Wisdom of Solomon 14.15 ; Epistle of Aristeas, 135 ; Sibyll. iii. 547, 554, 723.—Elements and celestial bodies : Wisdom of Solomon 13 ; Philo, *de decal.* 52 foll.—The tenacity of tradition is apparent from the fact that even Maimonides in his treatise of idolatry deals only with star-worship and image-worship. I know the treatise only from the Latin translation by D. Voss (in G. I. Voss's *Opera*, vol. v.).—Demons : Deuteron. 32. 17 ; Psalms 106. 37 ; add (according to LXX.) Isaiah 65. 11 ; Psalms 96. 5. Later writers : Enoch 19. 99, 7 ; Baruch 4. 7. Such passages as Jub. 22, 17 or Sibyll. prooem. 22 are possibly Euhemeristic.— Fallen angels : Enoch, 19.—Philo's demonology : *de gig.* 6–18, etc.

P. 128. St. Paul : 1 Cor. 10. 20 ; comp. 8. 4 and Rom. 1. 23.

P. 129. Image-worship and demon-worship not conciliated : *e.g.* Tertull. *Apologet.* 10–15 and 22–23, comp. 27.—Jewish demonology : Bousset, *Religion d. Judentums*, p. 326 (1st ed.).—Fallen angels : *e.g.* Athenag. 24 foll. ; Augustine, *Enchir.* 9, 28 foll. ; *de civ. Dei*, viii. 22.

P. 130. Euhemerism in the Apologists : *e.g.* Augustine, *de civ. Dei*, ii. 10 ; vi. 7 ; vii. 18 and 33 ; viii. 26.—Euhemerism and demonology combined : *e.g.* Augustine, *de civ. Dei*, ii. 10 ; vii. 35 ;

comp. vii. 28 fin.—Worship of the heavenly bodies : *e.g.* Aristid. 3 foll. ; Augustine, *de civ. Dei*, vii. 29 foll.

P. 131. Paganism a delusion caused by demons : Thomas Aq. *Summa theol*. P. ii. 2, Q. 94, art. 4 ; comp. below, note on p. 135.

P. 133. For the following sketch I have found valuable material in Gedike's essay, *Ueber die mannigfaltigen Hypothesen z. Erklärung d. Mythologie* (*Verm. Schriften*, Berlin, 1801, p. 61).

P. 134. Milton : *Paradise Lost*, i. 506. The theory that the pagan oracles fell mute at the rise of Christianity is also found in Milton, *Hymn on the Morning of Christ's Nativity*, st. xviii. foll.

P. 135. G. I. Voss ; *De Theologia Gentili*, lib. i. (published, 1642)— Voss's view is in the main that idolatry as a whole is the work of the Devil. What is worshipped is partly the heavenly bodies, partly demons, partly (and principally) dead men ; most of the ancient gods are identified with persons from the Old Testament. Demon-worship is dealt with in ch. 6 ; it is proved among other things by the true predictions of the oracles. Individual Greek deities are identified with demons in ch. 7, in a context where oracles are dealt with. On older works of the same tendency, see below, note on p. 140 ; on Natalis Comes, *ibid*. A fuller treatment of Voss's theories is found in Gruppe's work, § 25.—Thomas Aquinas : *Summa theol*. P. ii. 2, Q. 94, art. 4 ; comp. also Q. 122, art. 2.— Dante : Sommo Giove for God, *Purg*. vi. 118 ; his devils : Charon, *Inf*. iii. 82 (109 expressly designated as " dimonio ") ; Minos, *Inf*. v. 4 ; Geryon, *Inf*. xviii. (there are more of the same kind).— " Dei falsi e bugiardi " : *Inf*. i. 72. (Plutus, who appears as a devil in *Inf*. vii. was probably taken by Dante for an antique god ; but the name may also be a classicising translation of Mammon.)

P. 136. Mediaeval epic poets : Nyrop, *Den oldfranske Helte-digtning*, p. 255 and 260 ; Dernedde, *Ueber die den altfranzös. Dichtern bekannten Stoffe aus dem Altertum* (Diss. Götting. 1887).— Confusion of ancient and Christian elements : Dernedde, p. 10 ; the gods are devils : Dernedde, pp. 85, 88.—Euhemerism : Der-nedde, p. 4.—I have tried to get a first-hand impression of the way the gods are treated by the old French epic poets, but the material is too large, and indexes suited to the purpose are wanting. The paganism of the original is taken over naïvely, *e.g.*, by Veldeke, *Eneidt*, i. 45, 169.—On magic I have consulted Horst's *Dämonomagie* (Frankf. 1818) ; and his *Zauber-Bibliothek* (Mainz, 1821–26) ; Schindler, *Der Aberglaube des Mittelalters* (Breslau, 1858) ; Maury, *La magie et l'astrologie dans l'antiquité et au moyen âge* (Paris, 1860). These authors all agree that mediaeval magic is dependent on antiquity, but that the pagan gods are superseded by devils (or the Devil). The connexion in substance with antiquity, on which Maury specially insists, is certain enough, but does not concern us here, where the question is about the theory. In the *Zauber-Bibl*. i. p. 137 (in the treatise *Pneumatologia vera et occulta*), the snake Python is put down among the demons, with the remark that Apollo was called after it.—Magic formulae with antique gods : Heim, *Incantamenta magica* (in the *Neue Jahrbb. f. Philologie*, Suppl. xix. 1893, p. 557 ; I owe this reference to the kindness of my colleague, Prof. Groenbeck). Pradel, *Religionsgesch. Vers. u.*

Vorarb. iii., has collected prayers and magic formulae from Italy and Greece; they do not contain names of antique gods.

P. 137. Acosta : Joseph de Acosta, *Historia naturale e morale delle Indie*, Venice, 1596. I have used this Italian translation ; the original work appeared in 1590.—Demons at work in oracles : bk. v. ch. 9 ; in magic : ch. 25.

P. 138. Demon in Brazil : Voss, *Theol. Gent.* i. ch. 8.—Pagan worship in the Florentine and Roman Academies : Voigt, *Wieder-belebung d. klass. Altertums*, ii. p. 239 (2nd ed.) ; Hettner, *Ital. Studien*, p. 174.—On the conception of the antique gods in the earlier Middle Ages, see Gruppe, § 4.—Thomas Aquinas : *Summa theol.* P. ii. 2, Q. 94, art. 4.—Curious and typical of the mediaeval way of reasoning is the idea of seeking prototypes of the Christian history of salvation in pagan mythology. See v. Eicken, *Gesch. u. System d. mittelalt. Weltanschauung* (Stuttg. 1887), p. 648, and (with more detail) F. Piper, *Mythologie u. Symbolik d. christl. Kunst* (Weimar, 1847–51), i. p. 143 ; comp. also Gruppe, § 8 foll. Good instances are the myths in the *Speculum humanae salvationis*, chs. 3 and 24.—

P. 139. On Hebraism in general, see Gruppe, § 19 and § 24 foll. ; on Huet, § 28. Nevertheless, Huet operates with demonology in connexion with the oracles (*Dem. evang.* ii. 9, 34, 4).

P. 140. On Natalis Comes, see Gruppe, § 19. In bk. i. ch. 7, Natalis Comes gives an account of the origin of antiquity's conceptions of the gods ; it has quite a naturalistic turn. Nevertheless, we find in ch. 16 a remark which shows that he embraced demonology in its crudest form ; compare also the theory set forth in ch. 10. His interpretations of myths are collected in bk. x.— On Bacon, see Gruppe, § 22. Typhoeus-myth : introduct. to *De sapientia veterum*.—Alchemistic interpretations : Gedike, *Verm. Schriften*, p. 78 ; Gruppe, § 30. Of the works quoted by Gedike, I have consulted Faber's *Panchymicum* (Frankf. 1651) and Toll's *Fortuita* (Amsterd. 1687). Faber has only some remarks on the matter in bk. i. ch. 5 ; by Toll the alchemistic interpretation is carried through. Gedike quotes, moreover, a work by Suarez de Salazar, which must date from the sixteenth century ; according to Jöcher (iv. 1913) it only exists in MS., and I do not know where Gedike got his reference.—Thomas : *Summa*, P. ii. 2, Q. 172, arts. 5 and 6.

P. 141. Demonology as explanation of the oracles : see van Dale, *De oraculis*, p. 430 (Amsterd. 1700) ; he quotes numerous treatises from the sixteenth and seventeenth centuries. I have glanced at Moebius, *De oraculorum ethnicorum origine*, etc. (Leipzig, 1656).—Caelius Rhodiginus : *Lectionum antiq.* (Leyden, 1516), lib. ii. cap. 12 ; comp. Gruppe, § 15.—Caelius Calcagninus : *Oraculorum liber* (in his *Opera*, Basle, 1544, p. 640). The little dialogue is not very easy to understand ; it is evidently a satire on contemporary credulity ; but that Caelius completely rejected divination seems to be assumed also by G. I. Voss, *Theol. Gent.* i. 6.—Machiavelli : *Discorsi*, i. 56.—Van Dale : *De oraculis gentilium* (1st ed. Amsterd. 1683) ; *De idololatria* (Amsterd. 1696). Difficulties with the biblical accounts of demons : *De idol.*, dedication.— Fontenelle : *Histoire des oracles* (Paris, 1687). The little book has an amusing preface, in which Fontenelle with naïve complacency (and with a sharp eye for van Dale's deficiencies of style) gives an account of his popularisation of the learned work. On Fontenelle and the answer by the Jesuit, Balthus, see for further details Banier, *La mythologie et les fables expliquées par l'histoire* (Paris, 1738), bk. iii. ch. 1. Van Dale's book itself had called forth an answer by Moebius (included in the edition of 1690 of his work, *de orac. ethn. orig.*).—On the influence exercised by van Dale and Fontenelle on the succeeding mythologists, see Gruppe, § 34.— Banier : see Gruppe, § 35.

P. 143. Vico : *Scienza nuova* (Milan, 1853), p. 168 (bk. ii. in the section, Della metafisica poetica); political allegories, *e.g.* p. 309 (in the Canone mitologico). Comp. Gruppe, § 44.—Banier : in the work indicated above, bk. i. ch. 5.

P. 144. On the mythological theories of the eighteenth century, comp. Gruppe, § 36 foll. ; on Bryant, § 40 ; on Dupuis, § 41.— Polemic against Euhemerism from the standpoint of nature-symbolism : de la Barre, *Mémoires pour servir à l'histoire de la religion en Grèce,* in *Mém. de l'Acad. des Inscr.* xxiv. (1749 ; the treatise had already been communicated in 1737 and 1738); a posthumous continuation in *Mém.* xxix. (1770) gives an idea of de la Barre's own point of view, which was not a little in advance of his time. Comp. Gruppe, § 37.

P. 145. A good survey of modern investigations in the field of the history of ancient religion is given by Sam Wide in the *Einleit. in die Altertumswissensch.* ii. ; here also remarks on the mythology of older times. The later part of Gruppe's work contains a very full treatment of the subject.

INDEX

ABSOLUTE definitions of the divine, 16, 19, 68, 69, 82, 88.
Academics, 149.
Academy, later, 108, 114.
Acosta, 137, 139, 141.
Aelian, 121.
Aeneid (mediaeval), 136.
Aeschines, 93.
Aeschylus, 54, 55.
Aetolians, 97, 98.
Alchemistic explanation of Paganism, 140.
Alcibiades, 60.
Alexander the Great, 93, 112.
Allegorical interpretation, 104, 113, 139, 140, 143, 144.
American Paganism, 137, 139, 141.
Anaxagoras of Clazomenae, 7, 13, 25–29, 30, 31, 40, 62, 63, 66, 124.
Anaximenes, 30.
Angelology, 129.
Anthropomorphism, 14, 18, 19, 69.
Antisthenes, 13, 74, 109.
Apologists, 128, 130, 132, 139.
Arcisewsky, 138.
Aristides the Apologist, 129.
Aristides Rhetor, 121.
Aristodemus, 60, 62.
Aristophanes, 30, 32, 33, 39, 55, 56–58, 65.—Birds, 32.—Clouds, 30, 55, 56–58.—Frogs, 55.
Aristotle, 13, 30, 32, 46, 83–87, 104, 113.—Ethics, 84.—Metaphysics, 85–86.—Politics, 84.
Aristoxenus, 32, 33.
Asclepius, 111, 121, 126.
Asebeia, 6, 7, 8.
Aspasia, 27.
Atheism (and Atheist) defined, 1; rare in antiquity, 2, 133; of recent origin, 2, 143; origin of the words, 5; lists of atheists, 13; punishable by death in Plato's Laws, 77; sin of youth, 78.
Athene, 74.

Athens, its treatment of atheism, 6–8, 9, 12, 25, 39, 65 foll., 74, 75, 83, 86; its view of sophistic, 58–59.
Atheos (atheoi), 2, 10, 13, 14, 19, 23, 29, 43, 75, 110.
Atheotes, 2.
Augustine, St., 129, 135.
Augustus, 117; religious reaction of, 100, 113, 117, 120.
Aurelius, Marcus, 11, 121.

Bacon, Francis (De Sap. Vet.) 140.
Banier, 142, 143.
Bible, 130, 142.
Bion, 13, 109.
Brazil, 138.
Bruno, Giordano, 151.
Bryant, 144.
Buttmann, 152.

Caelius Calcagninus, 141.
Caelius Rhodiginus, 141.
Callicles, 48 foll., 63.
Carlyle, 112.
Carneades, 8, 108.
Cassander of Macedonia, 111.
Charon, 135.
Christianity, 126, 128–32.
Christians, their atheism, 9; prosecutions of, 10; demonology, 83.
Cicero, 19, 105, 114–17, 147.—Nature of the Gods, 115.—On the State, 115.—On the Laws, 115.—De consolatione, 116.
Cinesias, 60.
Copernicus, 151.
Critias, 13, 44–50.—Sisyphus, 44 f., 114.
Criticism of popular religion, 16, 17, 19, 35 foll., 74, 78, 82, 84, 88, 90, 99, 104, 109, 110, 122, 124–26.
Cuthites, 144.
Cynics, 74, 109–10, 122, 124, 147.
Cyrenaics, 75.

12